THANK YOU FOR DISRUPTING

THANK YOU FOR DISRUP TING

THE DISRUPTIVE BUSINESS PHILOSOPHIES OF THE WORLD'S GREAT ENTREPRENEURS

Jean-Marie **DRU**

WILEY

Published by John Wiley & Sons, Inc., Hoboken, New Jersey.
Published simultaneously in Canada.

For general information on our other products and services or for technical support, please contact our Customer Care Department within the United States at (800) 762–2974, outside the United States at (317) 572–3993 or fax (317) 572–4002.

Wiley publishes in a variety of print and electronic formats and by print-on-demand. Some material included with standard print versions of this book may not be included in e-books or in print-on-demand. If this book refers to media such as a CD or DVD that is not included in the version you purchased, you may download this material at http://booksupport.wiley.com. For more information about Wiley products, visit www.wiley.com.

Library of Congress Cataloging-in-Publication Data

Names: Dru, Jean-Marie, author.
Title: Thank you for disrupting : the disruptive business philosophies of the
   world's great entrepreneurs / Jean-Marie Dru.
Description: First Edition. | Hoboken : Wiley, 2019. | Includes index. |
   Identifiers: LCCN 2019011645 (print) | LCCN 2019019826 (ebook) | ISBN
   9781119575634 (Adobe PDF) | ISBN 9781119575665 (ePub) | ISBN 9781119575658
   (hardback)
Subjects: LCSH: Entrepreneurship—Case studies. | Businesspeople—Case
   studies. | Strategic planning—Case studies. | Corporate culture—Case
   studies. | Creative ability in business—Case studies. | BISAC: BUSINESS &
   ECONOMICS / Strategic Planning.
Classification: LCC HC29 (ebook) | LCC HC29 .D78 2019 (print) | DDC
   658.001—dc23
LC record available at https://lccn.loc.gov/2019011645

Printed in the United States of America

V10010018_050419

To Marie-Virginie
To my children
To my grandchildren

Contents

Introduction
Thank You for Disrupting

Thank You for Disrupting is about the entrepreneur as thinker. It's about how the most disruptive business builders in the world think and do things.

This book is not intended to relate their great achievements. Most of us have already heard or read about that. Rather, the intention here is to look behind these achievements to understand the big ideas and disruptive thinking that brought them into existence.

By fusing hardware and software 40 years ago, Steve Jobs was the first corporate leader who embodied, in an unprecedented way, the concept of "design thinking," which is today's dominant strategic framework. By launching the 1–1–1 philanthropic model,[1] Salesforce's co-founder Marc Benioff has become one of the most influential and outspoken voices on social issues, and has emerged as a corporate social responsibility ringleader. By creating, within the Haier company, over 2,000 independent teams[2] that have the liberty to talk directly with private equity firms, Zhang Ruimin has taken decentralization to an unimaginable level. By systematically disrupting existing HR policies, Patty McCord has forged Netflix's corporate culture, which is not only unique, but also emblematic of businesses born into the new economy. By rendering luxury accessible, while at the same time increasing the prestige of the LVMH brands,

Bernard Arnault has achieved a seemingly impossible task. He excels at managing creativity. By inventing a new business model for online journalism, Arianna Huffington has disrupted the conventional news delivery and made digital news reporting respectable. By being one of the first entrepreneurs in America to make social purpose and business work together, Sarah Breedlove was a pioneer in peer-to-peer marketing, community marketing, and cause marketing.

It's impossible to be exhaustive when devoting only a dozen or so pages to such avant-garde figures. I take a historical look at major disrupters from across the globe in recent decades. The reality is, the majority of them are men; but, fortunately, the business world is changing. I have no doubt that, in the very near future, more women will come forth as world-renowned disrupters.

Each domain of activity prompts fresh currents of thought. New concepts appear; paradigms emerge. Bodies of knowledge accumulate, collections of ever-evolving experience build up over time and are made available. It's true in science, where discoveries are made through challenging the mainstream thinking. It's true in art, where each period has seen new schools of thought arise, breaking with what former decades had celebrated. It's also true in political or social sciences, or in literature. In this way milestones are established, new directions given, tipping points created.

The same applies to the world of business. Business is an open forum where ideas circulate, where companies can continually inspire each other, and where people spread inspiration by moving from one company to another.

The 25 great entrepreneurs I talk about in this book have visions that extend beyond the frontiers of their business. In addition to the impact they have had on their own companies, they have also profoundly influenced the business world in general.

This is a celebration of truly disruptive spirits. To them, I say: *Thank you for disrupting. Thank you for advancing our collective thought process and making the world of business better and more interesting every day.*

PART

ONE

DISRUPTIVE
COMPANY
LEADERSHIP

Some of the leaders we discuss here come from the old business world, while others are part of the new landscape. All of them have left a mark that stretches beyond their own industries.

My goal is to recognize really disruptive business philosophies. They come from Steve Jobs, Jeff Bezos, Herb Kelleher, Bernard Arnault, Zhang Ruimin, and Jack Ma. All of them have refused to conform to rigid ways of thinking and acting. They have shown themselves to be free spirits, not limited by conventional thinking and not tolerant of any barrier to their goals. They all have the intrinsic qualities of great leaders: clear vision, technical competence, and the capacity to make quick decisions.

Steve Jobs laid the milestones of what will remain the most disruptive business model of our time. He built an innovative ecosystem and shaped what we have come to know as the New Economy. For many people, Apple's boss embodies the most brilliant and inventive spirit that the world of business has known. It would have been simply impossible to start with someone else.

CHAPTER 1

STEVE JOBS

ON USER EXPERIENCE, DESIGN AND TIMELESSNESS

When Steve Jobs passed away, Bill Gates said that Jobs's influence would be felt for "many generations to come."[1] Tim Cook, who succeeded Jobs at Apple, went even further, speaking of "thousands of years from now."[2]

History will remember Jobs for the seismic impact he had on the world of computers, especially in making them popular and accessible to all. What is also extraordinary is the way in which he was able to pivot his company several times. As Apple changed, so did its primary competitor: IBM, Microsoft, Samsung, in that order. Jobs's influence will mark the world forever, and his thinking will inspire hundreds of innovative business models.

In 1993, a book was published about Chiat\Day, the leading Californian agency that later became part of the TBWA network.

It was entitled *Inventing Desire*.[3] That's what Steve Jobs did. He invented tomorrow's desires.

All in One

When the iPod (and later the iPhone) came out, it was a real surprise not to find any instructions inside the package. Steve Jobs believed that users of his products should be able to use them instinctively. This might seem easy, but determining the most intuitive path requires a colossal amount of work. Jobs introduced what would be later called a "seamless user experience," known today as a "frictionless customer experience." Fluidity is the new norm.

At the launch of the Mac in 1984, Apple created an ad that referred to George Orwell's novel *1984*. Using the line "you'll see why 1984 won't be like 1984 . . ."[4] Apple introduced the concept that machines should adapt to humans, not the other way around. Today, the algorithm should adapt to the user. Technology should not be constraining, ergonomics must permit fluidity of interactions. This prefigures a future when we will be truly *augmented*, where our intimacy with a machine will be total. The result: a world without friction between man and machine.

From stores to products, from iPods to Macs, from iTunes downloads to iPad apps, Apple masters better than anyone what physicists call *the science of reciprocal actions*. Apple was the first to create an ecosystem where devices interact automatically with one another, where products work together "naturally." As we probably all remember, it started with the iPod. The iPod's initial pitch was very simple: "1,000 songs in your pocket," to quote the slogan on the billboards TBWA\Chiat\Day created for Apple. The offer was the combination of iTunes, the iTunes

Store, and the iPod. Photos, games, and apps came later, as users progressively adopted the platform.

Many companies around the world are now looking to create their own proprietary ecosystems, business models with elaborate architectures. Those in China are no exception. For example, hundreds of millions of Chinese have WeChat and Alipay. They use these all-in-one apps constantly to contact friends, pay bills, order taxis, reserve hotels and plane tickets, catch up on the news, or schedule appointments. In a *Fast Company* article about multifaceted "super apps," Albert Liu, EVP of Corporate Development at Veriphone declared, "The advantage of super lifestyle apps like Alipay or WeChat is they've connected incrementally more data than an app that's just focused on a single area. . . . There is no comparison with anything in the U.S."[5] WeChat is used on average more than 10 times a day for other things than chatting. It's been described as the "one app to rule them all." This all-in-one thinking is not so far from the mindset we inherited from Steve Jobs. And this approach is now driving the smartphone explosion in China.

Back in 1983, at the International Design Conference in Aspen, Colorado, Steve Jobs had already identified the huge potential of applications. A grand visionary, he predicted a future when each user would have "an incredibly great computer in a book that you can carry around with you and learn how to use in 20 minutes."[6] In 2007, the launch of the iPhone made all previous applications permanently outdated. Apps were presented for the first time as simple icons, accessible through a user-friendly tactile interface. In doing so, Steve Jobs created applications that were attractive and easy to use. Before then, no one could have thought that millions of apps would see the light of day in the next decade. Without the flair of Steve Jobs, and his drive to impose his vision of the future at all costs, Uber and Airbnb would probably never have existed. At least, they wouldn't exist in their current forms.

It was also in the early eighties that Steve Jobs pursued an idea that a number of his competitors disputed. As he put it, "More and more, software is getting integrated into the hardware. . . . Yesterday's software is today's hardware. Those two things are merging. And the line between hardware and software is going to get finer and finer and finer."[7] I remember some observers at the time castigating Steve Jobs for his desire to make Apple a company that integrated both hardware and software. In his critics' view, this would condemn the brand to a niche market. For a while, the naysayers' arguments were reinforced by the success of the seemingly absolute compatibility of Microsoft Windows. It's true that, at the beginning, Apple was the brand for a small core of believers, often from creative industries. These passionate brand advocates allowed Apple to carry on until the tipping point of 2001, which was when the iPod launched. That year Steve Jobs changed the world, opening up a new era for design.

Apple was an early adopter of what was already known as "design thinking," a both analytical and intuitive approach that leads to a deeper understanding of the user experience. Apple accelerated its emergence.

Today, all tech companies follow in the footsteps of Steve Jobs. Programmers are interested in not only what machines can do, but more importantly, how they are used. Fulfilling Jobs's predictions, the interaction between software and hardware has become the distinctive sign of business.

In the *Financial Times*, John Gapper commented on Google's project to make an entire platform—software and hardware—for driverless cars. He said, "Without the iPhone revolution, it is hard to imagine a technology company entering the transport industry, or designing a device that can steer cars around while receiving and transmitting streams of data."[8] The iPhone has provided tech companies with a new and unlimited world of opportunities. It was a pioneering product, helping people find ways to develop seamless hardware and software solutions that drive innovation into new spaces.

Only when hardware and software work perfectly together, can the user experience be optimized. And what is a strategy today if not to constantly seek to improve the user experience? That's why, little by little, as underlined by the *Harvard Business Review*, "Firms started treating corporate strategy as an exercise in design."[9] This approach facilitates the resolution of more and more complicated issues, addressing large-scale problems with multistep processes. Design helps cut through complexity.

For Steve Jobs, design was not so much a physical process as a way of thinking. This was the single-minded vision that drove his company. As a result, Apple took an end-to-end responsibility for the user experience years before the phrase "design thinking" became popular—and decades before the concept imposed itself on the business world as a whole.

The Art of Reduction

I would like now to talk not so much about design thinking, but of design in the usual meaning of the word. Jonathan Ive, who has for years been Apple's head of design, always adopted a minimalist approach. In our agency, we call this quest for simplicity "the art of reduction."

One of the key elements of minimalism resides in the dualism of simplicity and richness, the fact that clean forms allow the essential to be revealed. In search of immediate readability, minimalist art advocates no distance between the object and its purpose. Apple is a paragon of this philosophy. Any superfluous ornament or element is removed. Apple aims to show the object as an idea. This approach is the foundation of minimalist art.

Steve Jobs turned computers into objects of desire, making design matter. He educated billions of peoples' eyes. He made machines friendly and beautiful, brightening offices. By bringing beauty to a field where it was scarcely expected, Apple has raised our aesthetic expectations—forever, no matter the product category.

People talk about strong design like they talk about great art. Also like art, design leaves a lasting impression. Apple devices are art. Steve Jobs often said that he wanted Apple to be at the intersection of humanity and science. In almost every keynote presentation he made for the launch of a new product, he ended with a slide that showed two road signs at the intersection of Liberal Arts Street and Technology Street. It was his way of underlining how much he wanted to balance the humanities with science, creativity with technology, art with engineering.

Life Lessons

Steve Jobs's legacy is immense. First, he shaped what was to become the New Economy by rendering possible thousands of business models. Second, he helped make design an art in itself. There are, of course, many other things Steve Jobs accomplished, but I wish to close this chapter by remembering some of his observations, memorable thoughts on issues close to his heart.

On the subject of innovation, he confessed, "I'm actually as proud of the things we haven't done as the things I have done. Innovation is saying no to 1,000 things."[10] On simplicity, he stated, "Simple can be harder than complex: you have to work hard to get your thinking clean to make it simple."[11]

Steve Jobs did not leave us observations only of business, but also some timeless lessons from his own life and from life in general. He said that, for a free spirit like his, being fired by Apple was the best thing that could have happened. The liberty of becoming a beginner again replaced the burden of success. As he put it, "It freed me to enter one of the most creative periods of my life."

He loved to mix experiences, conjugate different disciplines. On this subject, he often said that it's impossible to connect the dots in advance. You can't predict how things are going to turn out. It's only with hindsight that you can make sense of things. "So, you have to trust that the dots will somehow connect in your future," he added.

In the famous commencement address he gave at Stanford, he told the graduating class that when he was 17, he learned to live each day as if it were his last. After all, one day it certainly would be. Jobs explained that since realizing this, each morning he looked at himself in the mirror and thought about whether he would be happy with what he was planning to do during the day, assuming that day would be his last. If the answer several days running was *no*, then he knew it was time to change something important.

In the same speech, he explained to the students, "Your time is limited, so don't waste it living someone else's life."[12] He pushed them to always aim higher, to stay hungry, to stay foolish. When I first saw the video of this speech, I was reminded of the script our agency created for the commercial "Think Different." In that we imagined Jobs saying:

> *Here's to the crazy ones. The ones who see things differently. . . . They're not fond of rules. And they have no respect for the status quo. . . . They push the human race forward. . . . And while some may see them as the crazy ones, we see genius. Because people who are crazy enough to think that they can change the world are the ones who do.*

This closely reflected Jobs's way of thinking. Perhaps the best way to sum up his passion to encourage each of us to "put a dent in the universe"[13] is with the famous question he asked John Sculley, whom Jobs was recruiting to be the president of Apple. It was 1985 and Sculley was the president of Pepsi when Jobs made him that offer. To make it impossible for Sculley to refuse, Jobs asked, "Do you want to sell sugar water for the rest of your life, or do you want to come with me and change the world?"[14]

CHAPTER 2

JEFF BEZOS

ON EXPERIMENTATION AND PLATFORMS

There are certain overused expressions that I am fed up with. For example, every company should be "client centric." This is hardly a new point of view; it has been around for decades. Back in the eighties, I remember the CEO of Auchan, one of Europe's leading retail chains, claiming to "put the client at the center" of all the strategies he developed for his group. Another worn-out management cliché is "the right to make mistakes." How many articles or books condescendingly exhort the importance of having courage and taking risks? As if businesspeople don't already know! These two platitudes in particular were staples of management books and articles, but when the Internet arrived, they were suddenly given new life.

In the digital revolution, everything starts with consumers; the Internet has truly put them at the center. Additionally, like it or not, companies are condemned to be resolutely open to risk.

The Internet is the catalyst for turbulence, leaving companies with no other choice than to constantly question themselves, to continually experiment, and to innovate at an accelerated pace. Otherwise, they run the risk of being left behind by competitors—and eventually disappearing.

Jeff Bezos is the person who best represents the resurgence of these two concepts, client centricity and risk-taking, in today's world. He has brought them to a new level of significance, which can be seen in Amazon. Bezos is driven to always get closer to his customers and he is constantly taking risks.

As a result, in 2017, Amazon was ranked number one in the American Customer Satisfaction Index[1] as well as in LinkedIn's ranking. Bezos has created the biggest and, above all, best service company in history; he calls Amazon "the earth's most consumer-centric company."[2]

Experimentation as a Strategy

The foundation to Jeff Bezos's thinking is that customers are never satisfied. They're always looking for a better way, but without a clear idea of what that may look like. This is why Jeff Bezos has always been dubious about customer research. He once declared that "a remarkable customer experience starts with heart, intuition, curiosity, play, guts, taste. You won't find any of it in a survey."[3] Jeff Bezos shares with Steve Jobs the belief that there's no point in asking consumers what they want. This goes against many business approaches. For example, the head of Xiaomi mobile phones constantly looks to improve his products based on feedback that is gathered daily from his user community. By contrast, Apple's and Amazon's visionaries believe that listening to consumers leads you nowhere. Bezos's goal is to give people what they don't know they need.

To invent, you obviously have to explore, experiment—take a leap into the unknown. Success comes out of conducting hundreds of unsuccessful experiments. There is always serendipity involved in discovery. Failure must be welcomed; it has to be embraced. In Silicon Valley this seems natural. Innovators there have even coined a word for it. They call failure *pivoting*.

"I've made billions of dollars of failure at Amazon,"[4] states Jeff Bezos. Recall the Fire Phone, the auction site Amazon Auction, and the hotel-booking site Amazon Destination. Dozens of ideas didn't work, but they were compensated by a few big successes. As he has said, Amazon's success depends on the number of experiments the company does per year, per month, per week, per day. For Bezos, experimentation is not a way toward the strategy; it *is* the strategy.

In technology, the return on investment can be very long tailed because the Internet increases the success of an idea exponentially. This leads Jeff Bezos to advise, "Given a 10 percent chance of a 100-times payoff, you should take that bet every time. But you're still going to be wrong 9 times out of 10."[5]

Experimentation means that decisions are no longer the result of lengthy upstream discussions. Rather, they are made after ideas have been tested live. This avoids unending talk, which is often counterproductive. When one project of many doesn't work out, it isn't seen as a mistake or a failure. To the contrary, it is seen as moving the company's collective thinking forward. Why? Because more failures actually lead to more successes. And "as the company grows, the size of the mistakes has to grow as well,"[6] Bezos has commented.

Amazon is always experimenting, so that customer experiences can become a little better every day. The goal is total satisfaction.

Experimentation is fueled by the desire to make the execution perfect. Attention is given to even the most minor details. But this is not micro-management. Like Steve Jobs, Jeff Bezos is obsessional when it comes to the quality of the user experience. This is why he personally controls every pixel on the site's landing page. During meetings, he spends most of his time reading emails from clients. He has declared that Amazon's customers remain loyal until the very second a competitor comes with a better service.

Jeff Bezos believes that this behavior sets him apart from the vast majority of other corporate leaders. He claims not to think about the competition because doing so would distract him from the essential: the consumer. Rather than thinking conventionally in terms of market share, Bezos thinks in terms of market creation. As he puts it, "Other companies have more of a conqueror mentality. We think of ourselves as explorers."[7]

The Platform Economy

Today, Amazon is perhaps the most influential company in the world, a position due to its unquestionable role as the spearhead of the platform economy. From now on, all companies will need to develop platforms, creating systems that interact easily with others.

What do Facebook, Twitter, Uber, Airbnb, Apple, Salesforce, and Amazon have in common? Their business models may be very different, but each owes its strength to an online platform that connects people and ecosystems. Of course, these businesses monetize their platforms differently. Facebook and Twitter live on advertising revenues. Uber and Airbnb charge fees. Apple sells products and has also built a platform for app developers, who, in turn, render the brand's products even more desirable.

These platforms are all sophisticated networks. Building them is complex because companies need to aggregate thousands and thousands of customers and the data that is relevant to them. Thanks to mobile apps, users can interact with any business, anytime, anywhere. The most valuable new-economy companies are all platforms that position them as quasi-monopolies.

When Jeff Bezos launched Amazon as a virtual bookstore, he devised an infrastructure that combined leading-edge IT with breakthrough logistics. This pairing became the core competency of his company. Amazon has since gradually built out from its initial assets. "Take inventory of what you are good at and extend out from your skills,"[8] advises Bezos. We have all witnessed Amazon's evolution from an e-commerce powerhouse to a company hosting third-party sites. Amazon Web Services makes its data expertise and cloud-computing capabilities available to thousands of other companies, including Netflix, to use in building their own applications. No one invests more energy than Amazon when it comes to improving, aggregating, and pivoting its business, or in helping clients pivot theirs. Unquestionably, Amazon has had a hand in the construction of the new economy. It has created a platform that is so sophisticated and powerful that it impacts the way the Internet works.

In its 2016 Tech Vision report, Accenture pointed out that "a platform does not just support the business, the platform is the business."[9] An interesting point in Accenture's analysis shows the degree to which digital platforms are not limited to tech companies. The health care sector includes many platforms that bring together different providers and collect and manage data via apps. This is also the case for other sectors of industry. General Motors has developed OnStar, a connected car platform,

Disney has its MyMagic+ platforms, and General Electric has created Predix, the world's largest industrial Internet of Things.

GE's clients can develop their own applications on the Predix platform. Their factories, as well as GE's, will be able to improve productivity through real-time data management and networking of industrial equipment. For instance, the wear and tear of machine tools will be constantly monitored, allowing maintenance needs to be predicted and serviced before problems occur. To take an example from another industry, it won't be long before every tracking point of every railroad company in the world is equipped with an electronic sensor that links to a real-time central database. This sets up industrial companies to become the next drivers of innovation.

According to Accenture, this will produce a major shift. Historical tech centers like Silicon Valley will disperse, spreading innovative activity across a variety of industry-concentrated global hubs. For General Electric and its former CEO Jeff Immelt, this will have a profound impact on the stock market. Immelt told *Le Figaro*, "Today, 20 percent of the S&P 500 market capitalization is represented by consumer Internet companies that didn't exist 20 years ago. I would bet that in the next 20 years the same will be true for industrial Internet companies."[10]

The open-platform era can be traced back to a famous internal memo that Jeff Bezos wrote in 2002. It contained six points. The fifth stipulated that: "All service interfaces, without exception, must be designed from the ground up to be externalizable. That is to say, the team must plan and design to be able to expose the interface to developers in the outside world. No exceptions." The sixth point toughly concluded that: "Anyone who doesn't do this will be fired."[11] Bezos's internal decree to Amazon ended up being applied throughout businesses. This is how Amazon taught other companies that, from now on, everything, or almost everything should be open.

Jeff Bezos practices what he preaches with the companies he acquires. His takeover of *The Washington Post* in 2013 is a good example. The results have been spectacular. And yet, it's hard to imagine two firms, Amazon and *The Washington Post*, with cultures that are further apart. Even so, this did not prevent Bezos's ways of thinking from infiltrating the daily newspaper with lightning speed. Since its acquisition by Bezos, *The Washington Post* has gone from being a newspaper to a news organizer. It now operates like a platform, a tech company, with journalism as its product. Engineers and developers work every day side by side with the editorial staff. Digital tools are at the core of the morning editorial conference. *The Washington Post* has become truly digital, with continuous 24-hour publication on the web. The content is distributed through a multiplatform system of which the newspaper is part. There are specific editorial processes that have been adapted to each platform. For instance, the Talent Network is an international network of freelance contributors that the *Post* can tap into when it needs additional or specialized reporting. Every day up to 400 stories can be published. The organization has developed metrics to qualify and monitor readers. It has also created incubator units to experiment with new ideas. *The Washington Post* also possesses its own set of digital tools, called Arc Publishing, which it sells to other media companies all over the world.

The turnaround has been remarkable. Key indicators—monthly unique visitors, subscriptions, digital revenues—have grown in double-digits over the past three years. *The Washington Post* has, at last, become profitable again.

Owning a newspaper is no easy venture. Donald Trump's attacks on the outlet (which he usually refers to as "Amazon's Washington Post"[12]) are virulent and occur almost daily. Taking criticism from another angle, Jeff Bezos has been rebuked by labor unions. Finally, journalists, even those at the *Post*, are increasingly mistrustful of Silicon Valley monopolies. Nevertheless, as one article from *Vanity Fair* pointed out, journalists in other media groups "are just looking for their Bezos. Everyone looks at *The Washington Post* under Bezos and is praying for the same."[13]

CHAPTER 3

HERB KELLEHER

ON HUMAN RESOURCES AND OPERATIONAL QUALITY

I remember hearing the French President François Mitterrand explain that qualifications were not essential when it came to hiring ministers and civil servants. Of course a necessary level of competence was required but, when bringing people on board, nothing was more important to Mitterrand than their frames of mind and their levels of commitment.

That was back in the eighties, at a time when I still believed in detailed job descriptions that specified the precise capabilities expected of candidates. Years later, I came across the famous phrase "Hire for attitude, train for skill,"[1] which was uttered by none other than Herb Kelleher, the founder of Southwest Airlines, a company with top performance in its sector.

Thousands of managers have tried to take Herb Kelleher's advice, more or less successfully, depending on the single-mindedness with which they have followed it. One well-known example is Tony Hsieh, the founder and CEO of Zappos. He followed Kelleher's guidance to the letter. Hsieh is convinced that happy employees put everything into giving their customers maximum satisfaction. He talks about "happiness management" and he has written a book about his approach called *Delivering Happiness.*

Employees First

"Employees first"[2] should not be seen as just a management adage or a sort of value-added accessory. This concept is at the very heart of Southwest Airlines' unmatched success. Naturally, the company's performance relies on its business model, which does not have a central hub, boasts the industry's fastest equipment rotation, and offers a single-class cabin. Yet, Southwest's flamboyant founder stressed that the airline's performance also owes a lot to the company's strong corporate culture and, in particular, to the priority given to its employees' fulfillment.

Over the past several decades we've witnessed the disappearance of carriers such as Pan Am, TWA, Eastern Airlines, Air America, Northwest Airlines, Pacific Southwest Airlines, and New York Air, to name but a few. At the same time, Southwest has seen its market capitalization grow twice as fast as the S&P 500. Its sales have reached $37.2 billion in 2017 and it employs more than 56,000 people. On top of all this, the company has never laid off a single employee since its creation in 1971, despite operating in a highly volatile industry.

The U.S. airline sector is often criticized for having unfriendly staff and mediocre service. Southwest is an exception. Its personnel, whether flying or on the ground, is seen as being open, concerned, always ready to do their best. This clearly comes from the company's "hire on attitude" philosophy. For candidates, character is given more importance than experience. Julie Weber, Southwest Airlines' HR director, makes a point of recruiting only people who have what she calls a "warrior spirit."[3] Our agency worked for Southwest and our people have witnessed that this is still the case. When Southwest Airlines recruits, they are not looking for the right experience, but for the right mindset.

Herb Kelleher believed that "the essential difference in service lies in minds, hearts, spirits, and souls."[4] This is the guiding line that defines Southwest's behavior. He thought that his company's culture gave it a real competitive advantage. The competition can buy physical things, but it cannot purchase the spirit of a company, which serves as an everyday inspiration to its employees. It's an asset that competitors cannot duplicate.

It's important to remember that Herb Kelleher imposed this point of view at a time when shareholder value (i.e., maximizing shareholders' equity) was the top priority among nearly all corporate boards. Optimizing earnings per share was supposed to drive all the company's strategies and initiatives. Herb Kelleher went against the grain. He was one of the first to invert the order of priorities and he summarized his thoughts in a brief manifesto: "Your employees come first. And if you treat your employees right, guess what? Your customers come back, and that makes your shareholders happy. Start with employees, and the rest follows from that."[5]

In return, what Herb Kelleher expected from his people was a perfect blend of energy, enthusiasm, team spirit, self-confidence, and tolerance of stress. He wanted the people in the company to think and act like entrepreneurs, like owners. Ann Rhoades, president and founder of the consulting firm People Ink, spent much of her career at Southwest Airlines, where she served as Chief People

Officer. When hiring, she used to ask applicants this intrusive question: "Tell me about the last time you broke the rules."[6]

The emphasis given to recruitment reminds me of the chief executive of another U.S. company. No matter what was on the agenda, he started every meeting by asking present staff the unnerving question: "Who did you recruit lately?"

Another primary value at Southwest Airlines is its famous sense of humor. Some Southwest flight announcements have gone viral on social media because they are so funny. The company believes humor is a great way to build bonds with its customers, so if you don't have a sense of humor, don't try to get a job at Southwest Airlines. I know of no other company that makes humor an essential requirement for recruitment.

This leads us to the most important point. By prioritizing its employees, Southwest Airlines provides a better quality of service, which has allowed it to be one of the first companies to disrupt the "low cost = low experience" equation. Herb Kelleher was one of the few who improved the status of low-cost services. He understood that low cost does not have to lead to compromises on quality. Since Southwest's success, many others have rushed into the path he traced. Low-cost companies now deliver great customer experience in every sector of activity: cars, hotels, banking, insurance, travel—the list goes on. A blogger[7] has recently stated that frugal has become the new cool.

Southwest's business model is truly virtuous. It would be easy to imagine that offering the best service at a lower cost would mean putting pressure on salary. At Southwest Airlines, the opposite is true. The company's employees are the best compensated in the airline industry. In addition to their salaries, they benefit from several forms of profit sharing and stock-option schemes. As a result, by placing staff interests ahead of shareholders' short-term returns, Southwest Airlines has maximized its long-term value for the benefit of its shareholders.

I've worked for more than 30 years with Michelin, a great French enterprise and a world leader in its domain. At first glance, Southwest Airlines and Michelin seem to be very different. Southwest Airlines was created in 1971, while Michelin was founded in 1889. But on the subject of respect for employees, the two companies have many things in common. Michelin is a company with irreproachable ethics and it has cultivated values like progress and trust for over a century. Very early on, the Clermont-Ferrand-based firm adopted a sense of corporate responsibility and has, from the outset, encouraged its people to act autonomously and to take initiatives. Like Japanese enterprises did decades later, Michelin has always given its workers and factory directors carte blanche to, respectively, look for ways of improving their machines and finding means of increasing productivity and quality.

At Michelin, there is no "Director of Human Resources." The position is still described the same way that it was in the 19th century: *directeur du personnel*. The current *directeur du personnel* is Jean-Michel Guillon. In an interview with *Le Figaro*, Guillon defended this title, even though he agrees it may sound old-fashioned and, as he describes, a bit "cheesy." Guillon also said Michelin will never change it. "Resources," he explained, "are used before being recycled or thrown away."[8] This cannot be the case with people. As he pointed out, the word *personnel* contains the word *person*.

Forbes[9] named Michelin America's Best Employer of 2018. Its category included the country's top 750 large and mid-sized employers. Michelin achieved a score of 9.90 out of 10. It was the only foreign firm in the top 10. The same year in France, Jean-Michel Guillon was elected Human Resources Director of the Year[10] (despite his actual title of *directeur du personnel*).

It is not surprising that, like at Michelin, the department in charge of staff at Southwest Airlines is not called the human resources department. Instead it is the People Department.

The Art Is in the Implementation

For many business leaders, setting the strategic direction is perceived as the noblest task. Executing action plans and tracking their evolution is often seen as an obligation that requires fastidious diligence. Academics and business writers have always given a preeminent place to strategy. Yet without operational excellence, it doesn't matter how clever the strategy is. What turns a strategy into a *winning* strategy is, without question, the operational quality—the execution.

As Peter Drucker said long ago, "Strategy is a commodity, execution is an art."[11] It's the execution over time that validates the strategy. The most successful company leaders are often acknowledged for their brilliant forward thinking. They would better be congratulated for their tenacity in implementing the chosen strategy and for the way they have piloted its execution.

Herb Kelleher certainly adhered to this point of view and liked to say, "We have a strategic plan. It's called 'doing things.'"[12]

He never allowed himself to become bogged down by too much strategic thinking or analysis paralysis. He believed that all he needed was an overall framework. Nothing more. And he came up with something very basic. For Southwest Airlines, his vision and the basis for this framework was simple: low cost, superior service, people first. This framework approach gives a long-term horizon. It liberates from the contingencies of the moment. It allows you to think with more agility. Walmart's CEO, Doug McMillon, agrees. He noted that, in the past, an organization like his "might have made big strategic choices on an annual or quarterly cycle. Today strategy is daily."[13] But he added that, for strategic thinking to be more fluid, managers needed to have an overall framework in mind. It doesn't need to be an elaborate strategy, but a simple guide.

Herb Kelleher's vision anticipated the new economy's way of doing things. Companies today do not try to develop a near perfect prototype because it takes too long. Instead, they advance step by step, through iterations. Strategy is no longer theoretical, conceived upstream. It is shaped progressively through the accumulation of experience. That is at the heart of the famous phrase "failing forward." Failing is necessary in order to learn, to progress, and to eventually succeed.

At a time when everything is created, deployed, and measured in real time, strategy and execution are one. Sequential thinking, which requires putting strategy first and execution second, is becoming more and more outdated, even irrelevant. Today's business relies on a constant back and forth between the two.

Herb Kelleher was among the first to get it—intuitively.

CHAPTER 4

BERNARD ARNAULT

ON THE MANAGEMENT OF CREATIVITY AND BRAND BUILDING

N early half of the luxury products in the world are bought by the Chinese. This includes things they purchase domestically and during trips abroad. This attests to the success of the "luxury for everyone" strategy adopted by LVMH, the world's leading luxury group.

LVMH Chairman and CEO Bernard Arnault is the third wealthiest man in the world. That is not an easy status to assume in France, where earning more than the average tends to raise suspicions.

I wish to talk about Arnault for three reasons. First, he has practically invented an industry, that of luxury. Second, it appears to me that no company is more competent than LVMH in managing intangible assets. Finally, he has created an organization that may survive all of the other enterprises mentioned in this book, given the longevity of luxury brands.

LVMH brings together the greatest number of prestige brands imaginable: Christian Dior, Louis Vuitton, Givenchy, Guerlain, Moët & Chandon, Hennessy, Berluti, Chaumet, Krug, Bulgari, Fendi, Céline, Emilio Pucci, Kenzo, Loewe, Loro Piana, Rimowa, Fred, Hublot, Zenith, and TAG Heuer among others—and that's without mentioning Le Bon Marché and Sephora. These brands have spent decades—if not centuries— forging their identities and reputations. They trace the full history of luxury. When Bernard Arnault acquired them, some of these brands were already the most prominent in their field. Others were sleeping beauties. Arnault breathed new life into them, and in doing so, built an empire.

LVMH is a staggering success. Bernard Arnault has grown an enterprise that it would be impossible to create today, given the scarcity of independent luxury brands and the cost of their acquisition, which is now exorbitant.

Sales of LVMH reached €42.6 billion in 2017, with a high level of profitability. With a market capitalization of €175 billion in March 2019, it leads the French Stock Exchange. The group employs nearly 145,000 people. And the company's philosophy is encapsulated in this phrase, which appears in one of its annual reports: "We are a natural alliance between art and craftsman- ship where creativity, virtuosity and quality interact."[1]

Art and Commerce

LVMH's brands are not just brands. They are called *houses*: the House of Louis Vuitton, the House of Moët & Chandon, the House of Guerlain. LVMH is a federation of 70 houses that are all, in their particular domains, ambassadors of a certain refined *art de vivre*. Each possesses its own cultural identity, but they share an aura of exclusivity, a sense of an elite offering, and an image of distinction.

The luxury industry has always been close to the art world and LVMH is no exception. The company forms partnerships with the greatest artists of our time, such as Jeff Koons, Takashi Murakami, and many, many others. LVMH's designers are also true artists in their own right. The group has become a cross-roads where the great designers of the world converge.

To develop LVMH's houses, Bernard Arnault has always had the flair and sensitivity to find the right designer, the great creative talent who fit naturally with each house's spirit. He also knew how to create exceptional teams, partnering these great creative talents with top-flight business minds. This, too, required real know-how. When art and business come together seamlessly, success follows. Many years have gone by since Pierre Bergé and Yves Saint-Laurent showed the way at Saint-Laurent, a competitive house. Ten years ago, John Galliano and Sydney Toledano brought success to Dior and, today, Nicolas Ghesquière and Michael Burke lead the way at Louis Vuitton.

All of this bears testimony to a unique savoir faire. It could be described as the *management of creativity* and management of the highest order, that of a very big group.

Bernard Arnault has created a specific organization in order to deliver this. The company is both decentralized and vertical, which might at first appear to be a contradiction in terms. LVMH is made up of a large number of small enterprises, which, before joining the group, were often family owned and very independent, but lacking in resources to expand globally. To succeed, Bernard Arnault has encouraged them to maintain their entrepreneurial spirit, keeping them agile and responsive. Their limited size allows their management to stay closely in touch with all the staff, in particular the craftspeople, who occupy key positions. Houses remain autonomous in their creative processes. They appear independent, but, obviously, they are not.

While the group is not organized in a typical pyramid structure, Bernard Arnault has applied vertical integration in all the sectors where it makes sense, from sourcing to retailing. One analyst went as far as comparing the organizational structures of LVMH and General Motors. The parallel between the two may seem somewhat incongruous, but a closer look reveals that they have much in common. Unlike Ford and Chrysler, General Motors has succeeded in maintaining a stable of brands since the 1950s. Like the houses of LVMH, GM brands like Cadillac, Chevrolet, and Pontiac each enjoy a certain autonomy. To make this possible, the group had invented new techniques of vertical management combined with mutualization, a combination that ended up being an example for industries all over the world.

As with Steve Jobs, Jeff Bezos, and Herb Kelleher, Bernard Arnault is the keystone of his enterprise. He is the sole captain at the helm. Even if each house believes itself to be master of its own destiny, Bernard Arnault's approval is paramount. He will never sanction a project or idea that could damage LVMH brands' intangible capital. This explains his extreme attention to detail, a concern that, in other companies, would not fall upon the chief executive. He takes personal interest in the fabrics, materials, cuts, and all those subtle characteristics of the pieces and creations he endorses. And over time he has forged a very discerning eye.

This attention to detail reminds me of Apple's chief design officer, Jonathan Ive. When Apple was building its first store in New York City, Ive required the blocks of marble to be first sent to the Cupertino headquarters so he could inspect their veining.

All the minute details under the surface of an Apple product indicate what craftsmanship means on an industrial level. The insides of Apple's products, the parts we never see, are given as much attention as the outside. The uncompromising culture of Swiss watchmaking has rubbed off on Silicon Valley.

Steve Jobs used to meet with our Los Angeles agency once a week, each Wednesday, from 10 a.m. to noon. He insisted on maintaining close involvement because everything we did mattered to the brand. He was first and foremost interested in ideas, but this did not stop him from scrutinizing the copy for a print ad or from personally choosing a picture to be used in Apple Stores.

Our Paris agency presented film projects to Bernard Arnault on several occasions. Each time, he showed himself to be interested in not only the script and choice of models, but also in the decor, the accessories, the lighting, and the music. I was not always in full agreement with his comments, but his level of involvement has always impressed me. It reveals the level of implication required in the industry in which LVMH operates. God is in the details.

In a word, I would say that Bernard Arnault gave to the management of creativity its true status. In the book, *La Passion Créative*, published 20 years ago, he said that his job consists of "creating an economic reality out of the ideas coming from all the creators in the group."[2] As such, Arnault also sees himself as a creator, which he is.

The Luxury Industry as Model

Let's now discuss the marketing of luxury brands. I do not use the expression "brand building" here because most of these brands have been built over decades. I'll consider rather how to make them blossom, how to increase their value over time, and how to render them ever more desirable.

A common trait among luxury brands is to embrace opposites. They navigate between paradoxes and they thrive on contradiction. They must nourish themselves from the past and also look into the future, surrounding themselves with innovation and inventing the currents of tomorrow. Luxury brands seek to attract attention, yet at the same time remain aloof. They address a narrow, elitist audience, but they want to be celebrated by everyone. They produce limited-edition items to create a state of rarity, whereas companies in other sectors do everything to keep their products in stock. They raise their prices and, at the same time, sell larger and larger volumes. Luxury brands have hence increased their revenue to the level of mass-market industries, but they have never fallen into the trap of being ordinary. So many paradoxes permit them to remain exclusive.

Luxury indeed possesses very different, if not antithetical, characteristics from the mass market. And yet, I believe it could be helpful for mass-market brands to understand how luxury brands think. Traditional marketing employs positioning to best exploit mass media. This approach reduces a product's argument to a single salient idea, something that instantly sticks in the mind. Only one thought can be effectively communicated in 30 seconds, so brands have to choose a single direction, renouncing other aspects. Luxury brands do not choose. They want to be everything. They reside at the heart of a subtle web, where complexity is a virtue.

To go further on this topic of marketing high-end products, it is interesting to compare the approaches of LVMH, L'Oreal, and Procter & Gamble. LVMH is one of the jewels of French industry; L'Oreal is another. LVMH is the leading luxury goods company in the world, while L'Oreal is the number-one beauty company. Both are very different, and yet they share certain cultural elements. L'Oreal, like LVMH, knows how to blend product performance—the efficacy of its skin care products— with symbolic and metaphoric brand universes. In some markets, such as fragrances, L'Oreal is in direct competition with LVMH. And, thus, a mass-market company like L'Oreal is progressively adopting the codes of the luxury industry.

Nearly 35 years ago, another consumer goods company, Procter & Gamble, decided to challenge L'Oreal's leadership position. After acquiring Oil of Olay in 1985, P&G went on to buy a number of beauty brands, including Betrix and Max Factor and German hair-care brand Wella. I remember Ed Artzt, the chief executive at the time, telling me what a predominant place the beauty business was going to occupy at Procter & Gamble. P&G was leader in every category it operated in, so he thought the company would naturally dethrone L'Oreal to become number one of the worldwide beauty market. . . . Three decades later, in 2016, P&G's renouncement was spectacular. The company sold more than half of its activities in the sector.

There are several possible explanations for this. I would like to dwell on just one that is not often mentioned by other observers, but to me appears essential. Procter & Gamble, like all consumer goods companies, is driven by the quantitative. I would go so far as to say that, at P&G, whatever cannot be measured is practically considered nonexistent. This evidently constitutes a barrier to imagination and creativity. Conversely, at L'Oreal, the quantitative does not prevail over the qualitative, the intangible is crucial. Its people don't hesitate to open themselves up to things of an artistic or intuitive nature, even within the context of their jobs.

I was invited to Cincinnati in the nineties to give a presentation on L'Oreal's approach to marketing. The fact that I am French might have given P&G's management the impression that I knew a little about L'Oreal's specific ways of doing things. During our discussions, I was able to measure the distance that separated L'Oreal and P&G. I was struck by the fact that the people in the two companies did not give the same importance to the same things. Far from it. Form, execution, and style are essential elements for L'Oreal. They contribute to the brand essence. At the time, this was less the case at P&G. Anyway in the long run, L'Oreal managed to keep Procter & Gamble at bay.

Many mainstream brands are now trying to move upscale and enter the premium area. Often, this is because they are looking to penetrate market segments with higher margins. Such a move requires managers to change their habits. Rather than only focusing on their products' functional performance, they must also take into account the symbolic values of their brands. They need to avoid being excessively rational and learn to trust their intuition.

By *intuition* I don't mean superficial flashes of brilliance, but rather a combination of impressions and experiences that suddenly rise to the surface to form a brand idea or a brand territory. Intuition is an incomparable driver. It is the lifeblood of the luxury industry. Bernard Arnault was once described by *Le Figaro* as "the intuitive businessman par excellence."[3]

In the final analysis, it is a unique blend of business acumen and intuition that counts. On this, Bill Bernbach, the most famous adman of the last century, said, "Knowledge is ultimately available to everyone. Only true intuition, jumping from knowledge to an idea, is yours and yours alone."[4]

CHAPTER 5

ZHANG RUIMIN

ON DECENTRALIZATION AND
CUSTOMER-CENTRICITY

Zhang Ruimin has run Haier for 35 years. This world-renowned Chinese company sells white goods in a very mature market where products are most often commoditized. Perhaps because of this Zhang has adopted and even invented completely new management practices. Indeed, he has dramatically shaken up the organization of his company several times and, in doing so, he has accomplished something that might have been more expected of a leader in the new economy.

For Zhang, companies that fail to disrupt themselves are condemned to be disrupted by others. It is inconceivable to him that a company can eternally depend on the same business model. One day or another, it will find itself obliged to self-disrupt.

Zhang has forced himself to reinvent his company, continuously. This former Red Guard and civil servant was inspired by American and Japanese business literature. The works of Peter Drucker, Gary Hamel, and Kenichi Ohmae no longer hold secrets for Zhang, who was a serious business student. As a business leader, he applies the most pertinent ideas, following them to the letter. He complains that active sources of inspiration are drying up. According to him, American theoretical thinking is now at a standstill.

At Haier, Zhang sought to invent the company of the future. It proved to be an arduous task. The company he took over was provincial in scope, making products that were often defective. He had to fight against two very different aspects of Chinese culture. On the one hand was the heritage of Confucius, which consecrates harmony and the cult of ancestors. Those practices and beliefs could favor stagnation. On the other hand were the vestiges of the Cultural Revolution, which had led to a certain chaos inside the factories and to a disregard of quality standards. At Haier, as elsewhere, a lack of discipline was the norm. Anything and everything went.

Haier has known three distinct periods under Zhang's leadership. Each time, he totally changed the organization of one of the oldest collective firms in the country. First of all, he transformed a company making low-quality goods into one cited not just in China but also throughout the world for the irreproachable quality and reliability of its products. From the year 2000 on, he began building a global brand by exporting products Haier manufactured in China and then producing them in the new factories Haier built from Southeast Asia to South Carolina. The company has since become the world's largest seller of washing machines, refrigerators, air conditioners, and other major appliances. With 2017 global revenues of $37.2 billion, it is well ahead of its American and Swedish rivals, Whirlpool and Electrolux. Finally came Haier's most recent and maybe most significant phase: evolving from a manufacturer of goods to a service provider—in every sense of the word.

Managing through self-disruption is Zhang's trademark, an approach that makes him and his company stand out from the crowd. One story in particular illustrates Zhang's emphasis on product quality. It has become a legend in the world of Chinese business. After a customer complained about a broken refrigerator, which he brought back to the factory, Zhang checked the entire stock of 400 refrigerators, looking for a replacement. In doing so, he discovered a total of 76 defective refrigerators. He then selected 75 employees and asked them what they should do with the faulty machines. Some suggested selling them at a discount, while others recommended giving them away to Haier employees. Zhang grabbed a hammer and destroyed one of the faulty refrigerators, ordering each of his stunned employees to do the same. Then he said, "We cannot expect to smash refrigerators every day. But actually, I think about doing it every day."[1] That singular act of destruction impressed on employees that poor quality would no longer be acceptable.

Just imagine the impact of this gesture in a country where, at the time, a refrigerator could cost nearly as much as a worker's annual salary. This event became a cult moment in the company's history and was a tipping point on its path toward quality. The hammer is now on display, like a relic, in the company museum near its Qingdao headquarters.

This was the first step in a long journey that made Haier a model for Chinese companies and, judging by the press coverage of its success, for the rest of the world, too.

Everyone Is a CEO

Haier's history is one of a culture in constant evolution, of an organizational model always being challenged. Zhang relies on a simple observation: Companies rarely know how to get the best out of their employees, which leads to consequential waste. This is why he is always looking for organizational models that allow his people's talent to be best expressed—and supported.

Haier puts responsibility at the very heart of its culture. The degree of autonomy given to employees at the lowest part of the hierarchy is far greater than even in the most forward-thinking Western companies. Haier comprises over 2,000 autonomous units, each one operating as a small business. These micro-companies are responsible for their own P&L and include between 20 and 30 employees from sales, finance, logistics, and marketing. The rest of the company—Haier employs 80,000 people—supplies resources to these autonomous units on a contractual basis and is paid for the services it provides.

Any employee can propose a new idea, be it a simple product improvement, a true innovation, a new service, or a better process. Employees vote on whether an idea should be put into practice. For ideas that pass muster, the person who proposed it becomes the project leader. The project leader selects the team that will undertake the venture. In this manner, Haier's business units operate just like start-ups. The team will last for the duration of the project, which could vary from six months to two years. Should team members feel their leader is underperforming, they can request a new leader, someone they can elect themselves.

At Haier, compensation is directly linked to individual performance. Every day staff members are awarded points; the amount depends on their contribution. At the end of the month, points and other awards are added up, while penalties are subtracted. The final number is used to calculate an employee's pay. This draconian approach would obviously be difficult to import to the West. But what is interesting, as states Peter Hinssen in *Forbes*, is that:

> Basically what Zhang Ruimin did, was to create a culture of entrepreneurship inside his company by copying and transferring the rules of the outside market inside his company. He thus created a network of small "companies" competing against one another inside Haier and made sure that the remuneration depended on the end-users.[2]

This has led to a highly competitive, but also quite uncomfortable environment. And yet, virtually all the employees accept it. Haier is also one of the most attractive companies for young graduates because the company allows them to believe they could grow there better than anywhere else.

What Zhang has succeeded in creating is a bold and innovative organization within a traditional commodity manufacturer. Haier is a company built with extraordinary precision and on a scale never before attempted. Staff members are not simple employees content to receive and execute their superiors' orders. They are entrepreneurs who feel they are their own bosses. They have become CEOs of their own, as stated in internal company documents. This organizational innovation is like a "bottom-up liberation."[3]

In this structure, the uncommon becomes typical. For instance, Zhang goes as far as encouraging his micro-unit leaders to seek out venture capital firms to co-finance their innovative ideas. That is further proof that the independence of these micro-units is not just for show. So far, no fewer than 200 teams have raised venture capital this way, which would obviously be unimaginable in Western companies.

Haier's model rendered middle management obsolete, so Zhang removed it from the organization. In 2013, he fired 10,000 middle-management staff.[4] As a result, control by upper-level management tightened. Upper management's role is to define the company's overall direction, to set performance standards, and to provide frontline employees with the resources they need. The employees' achievements are measured daily. Performance indicators are multiple, comprehensive, and thorough. There are detailed three-year, yearly, quarterly, monthly, weekly, and even daily plans. Staff members are briefed on results from the previous week in order to plan for the next one and the six that follow. Inspired by Japanese management books, Zhang has introduced processes that allow the control of everything, everyone, and every day.

This level of control might at first appear to undermine the independence of his employees, but a closer look reveals that the opposite is true. As Bill Fischer said in *Reinventing Giants*, "optimal innovation occurs at the moment when team members believe that they have absolute freedom to contribute their talents, and management believe that it is in complete control—both at the same time."[5]

In addition to the pairing of freedom and control, Haier thrives on another paradox: complexity and agility. On the one hand, Haier's organization is far from simple. It is constantly becoming more complex. But on the other hand, having thousands of autonomous units injects great agility into the enterprise. This is not the least of the Haier model's contradictions.

Many observers believe that Zhang is one of those entrepreneurs that will have a profound effect on business worldwide. Time will tell. But it's already clear that he has been able to impose an enormous cultural change on an enterprise that, at one time, could not have been more traditional. He innovated in a way that Western firms often do not, in the organization of the company.

Reading about and observing Zhang can give one the feeling that the corporate organizational structure of the future will come from China. For more than a century and a half, all over the world, companies have been organized in departments, each given a precise function: research and development, production, marketing, sales, logistics, sourcing, human resources, finance. This seems immovable, cast in stone. At Haier, these functions still remain, but they have broken free from the confinement of the typical organizational structure. Gone are the silos of function and department. Everything has become interdisciplinary.

In the West, when innovation is discussed, it is most often in terms of products, services, and business models. Organizational redesign is not typically part of the conversation. Yet, it is probably from this field that managerial insights will emerge in China in future years. This is one of the contributions China will bring to the rest of the business world.

The system Zhang has put into place is intended to liberate the talent of his employees, get the very best out of each individual, and avoid waste in HR management. Zhang often quotes Peter Drucker, one of his greatest influences: "The purpose of an organization is to make ordinary people do extraordinary things."[6]

Zero Distance with the Customer

To follow up on the story of Zhang and the hammer, I'd like to share this telling anecdote about a potato. A client from the Chinese countryside complained that his washing machine was not working. Haier's local technician discovered that the client was also using the machine to clean freshly unearthed potatoes. He informed headquarters, where Haier's engineers saw the opportunity to satisfy other customers; this client was surely not alone in how he used his washing machine. They conceived the first-ever machine designed to wash not only clothes but also vegetables. At the beginning, the new machine, equipped with oversized pipes, provoked incredulity, especially outside of China. But since its launch, Haier has sold over half a million of them. And it happened because the company listened so carefully to one of its customers. Zhang takes this to the point of obsession.

Zhang explains that he has turned a manufacturing company into a customer-oriented organization. It may sound trivial because most, if not all, companies aspire today to be customer-centric. Yet many fall well short of that ambition. At Haier, practically all the employees are in contact in one way or another with the customer. Haier thinks of itself as a service company, and service is best provided when, as its chief executive insists, there is "zero distance with the customer."[7]

This is the other reason for Zhang to decentralize his company to such an unheard-of extent. Without this type of organization, he would not have been able to achieve his goal of zero distance. Every unit, every employee is connected to the consumer through what he calls "a market chain." To quote Bill Fischer:

> Employees form a chain of internal customers at each successive downstream activity as well. The design department, for example, is a customer of the environmental testing laboratory, product divisions are customers of the technical facilities department, and managers and employees are the customers of Haier University for staff training. These internal transactions work as in a marketplace.[8]

This profound decentralization, combined with the will to annihilate the distance between employees and their customers, has made Haier the most innovative company in its sector. Its list of innovations is staggering. In addition to washing machines that also rinse vegetables, Haier has produced shrunken fridges for students, an anti-shock water heater, a deep freezer that works without power for 100 hours, a wash basin–mirror unit that custom warms water via facial recognition, and a TV monitor integrated into headphones that allows a user to program the television through brain waves. Zhang wants Haier to become "a giant incubator of innovations."[9]

As for the machine that rinses potatoes, it inspired the technology for a washer that does laundry without soap, launched by Haier in 2009. This truly disruptive technology has enabled Haier to progressively become the leading supplier to laundries in China before moving on to the rest of the world.

Forbes published an article about Zhang called "Wisdom from the Oracle of Qingdao."[10] His prophecy has been fulfilled. The Chinese authorities, his fellow leaders, his staff, and journalists all believe Zhang is the model to follow. He has made his dream come true; Haier is really a worldwide brand—the first to emerge from China.

CHAPTER 6

JACK MA

ON CHINESE BUSINESS MODELS AND DISRUPTIVE MANAGEMENT

In China, November 11 is Singles' Day. Originally called Bachelors' Day, it began in the late nineties when students invented a special day for singles. The date, written as 11–11, is very popular among young Chinese. It has become an opportunity for them to meet and party with friends.

In 2009, Chinese e-commerce giant Alibaba turned this party day into a mammoth annual "Global Shopping Festival." Calling it an "anti-Valentine's Day," the company renamed it Double 11, a term[1] it invented and trademarked.

The festival has since become the world's largest 24-hour shopping event, supported by Alibaba's unique global cloud, logistics, and payment infrastructure. In 2018, 180,000 brands participated in Double 11, including thousands of foreign ones. Hundreds of millions of consumers made purchases through

Alibaba's platform. The online retailer sold $30.8 billion worth of merchandise, making the event bigger than Black Friday and Cyber Monday combined. At one point, more than 350,000 orders per second[2] were being registered. An Alibaba spokesman commented, "It's like the Olympics or the Super Bowl of e-commerce."[3]

This event bears testimony to the extraordinary rise of Alibaba and its founder and chief executive, Jack Ma. His success story fascinates media outlets across the world. There is certainly a lot to be learned from this former English teacher, who claims to know nothing about technology. In spite of, or perhaps thanks to, this background, Ma has built a huge technology empire. Nothing seems impossible to "Crazy Jack,"[4] as he is affectionately known in the Internet world.

Alibaba and its subsidiaries account for approximately 80 percent of all of China's e-commerce business. *Fortune* magazine described it as "the equivalent of Amazon, eBay, and PayPal combined."[5] Its global revenue has seen exponential year-over-year growth and totaled $39.9 billion in 2017.

A Contrarian Model

Jack Ma has shown great resilience. He is at the head of a company that, like Haier, has reinvented itself on several occasions. He often quotes the founder of Intel, Andy Grove, who said "only the paranoid survive."[6] Jack Ma is well positioned to know. Maintaining a healthy level of paranoia is essential in the tech world, where a new idea, business model, or app can provoke an industry shift that renders current business models instantly obsolete, from one day to the next.

Alibaba started out as a business-to-business service provider, created to help Chinese companies find export channels online. It then progressively began to connect entrepreneurs with global markets, wherever they were. The concept allowed, say, a mid-sized Norwegian company to sell more effectively in Brazil. But faced with the threat of the arrival of eBay in the Chinese market, Jack Ma launched Taobao. This entry into the consumer world was initially a defensive move. With 666 million monthly active users, this online shopping website now dominates e-commerce in China. Other initiatives soon followed, beginning with the launch of Alipay, the online payment app. Processing more than 175 million daily transactions[7] and 54 percent of all electronic payments in China, it is by far the biggest online payment service provider in the world.

Alibaba owes its unheard-of success to the power of its unique business model. And also to the discovery of a real consumer insight. In China, most consumers were initially mistrustful of the digital world because it was unfamiliar. Chinese suppliers hesitated to sell things online because they worried that customers would not pay. This was the insight that led Jack Ma to create Alipay. Alipay's main feature consists of freezing the money. It's an escrow payment system. Vendors are reassured they will be paid for the products they ship. At the same time, consumers know that if they pay with Alipay, their account will only be debited once they are satisfied with the goods they have received.

Alibaba is intent on gaining control over the virtual wallet, in particular against Tencent, China's leader in messaging and gaming, thanks to its more than one billion monthly active users. Alipay is an incomparable asset for Alibaba in this context. It now handles close to a trillion dollars a year in online transactions, three times that of PayPal. Jack Ma always thought that finance must be disrupted, which is exactly what he did with Alipay.

Alibaba's websites are designed to reflect Chinese culture. They are packed with all sorts of information and graphics that clash with the clean styles of Amazon or Google. For Westerners, it all looks a bit messy. You need to scroll down several times to see the whole page. The impression of chaos is reinforced through discovering the most improbable products on Alibaba's sites, stuff usually found in local street markets. Thousands of small, even tiny companies, as well as millions of individuals from the back of beyond, in the remotest of Chinese villages, were given the opportunity to make money online. Most of them owe the very existence of their businesses to Alibaba. All this contributes to making its sites look like a gigantic online hardware store. From the outset, Alibaba's websites were intentionally built differently. They are made in China, for the Chinese.

This reminds me of Big Bazaar's amazing success in India. Its founder Kishore Biyani came to the conclusion that the basic principles behind successful retail in developed economies just didn't work in India. All those look-alike stores filled with long, pristine aisles, tidy shelves, air-conditioning, clean graphics, and skilled staff made Indians feel that they couldn't afford the products on display. So Kishore Biyani transformed his stores into huge local markets: bazaars. Garish colors prevail. People bump into each other. They bargain just like in a street stall. Today Big Bazaar is India's most popular supermarket chain. Its president loves saying "we can only survive in chaotic environments."[8] He knows what he is talking about. He had previously encountered spectacular failure by following management consultants' advice to model his stores on Walmart and Carrefour.

Not adapting to local market characteristics proved fatal to eBay's success in some countries. Its website design faithfully followed the American model, and the Chinese were uncomfortable with it. It was one of the main reasons for eBay's amazing failure in China.

Jack Ma's unorthodox way of doing things manifests itself from the top to the bottom of his company, in whatever the area. I have retained two examples of this. First, when Alibaba's sales suffered during the global financial crisis in 2008, Ma decided to lower subscriber fees by 60 percent for those who signed up for a broader range of services. As Duncan Clark points out in *Alibaba: The House That Jack Ma Built*,[9] the financial world reacted very badly. With sales down, they hardly expected the company to drastically reduce the cost of membership. An increase seemed more appropriate for the situation. From one day to the next, a large proportion of Alibaba's revenue was put in jeopardy. This was evidently a risky strategy and quite the opposite of what many envisioned. But Jack Ma had anticipated that a rise in sales would offset the subscription price cut. This is exactly what happened. And it heralded a totally new period for Alibaba, resulting in more sales of value-added services, which have since become its major motor for growth.

A second example of Jack Ma's unconventional way of doing things is illustrated by the fact that he once told his staff to sell some of the shares they owned in the company. I'm not aware of any other chief executive who has done this. Jack Ma believed that the people who worked so hard for the company, and whose jobs often kept them away from their loved ones, deserved to be rewarded—along with their families. In September 2014, Alibaba made the largest stock market flotation in history. The surge of the share price valued the company at $230 billion. Jack Ma told his employees, "Selling the stock doesn't mean you don't like the business. I encourage you to sell some, to build your life, to give a reward to your family."[10]

Many observers talk of Jack Ma's contrarian mind. It's true that a lot of his initiatives go against the grain of conventional Western habits. They echo what was referred to in the 1990s as contrarian marketing. I remember being critical of this kind of approach back then. In my book *Disruption*, published in 1996, I noted that "you can oppose something without proposing its opposite."[11] At the time, contrarian marketing seemed too simplistic to me, but I must admit that seeing Jack Ma's success with it has led me to reconsider. Whatever the subject, it's worth asking whether, at a given point in time, an approach that is diametrically opposed to conventional practices could prove fruitful.

Embracing Change through Paradox

Later in this book I will examine in more detail paradoxes, those contrary elements that all business leaders must manage. They are sources of tension, but at the same time they can serve as a positive platform for inspiration. Mastering paradox is a characteristic of great industry leaders.

For example, Jack Ma knows how to walk the fine line between chaos and order. On the one hand, he loves to say, "If you plan, you lose. If you don't plan, you win."[12]

In practice, his company doesn't follow a three- or five-year plan. But this doesn't stop Jack Ma from believing in rigor and discipline. In *China's Disruptors*, Edward Tse quotes Alibaba's chief strategy officer as saying:

> Alibaba is constantly looking for the right combination of opportunity and competence—where we can bring together the biggest opportunity and the most important leverage point. We don't jump randomly, we do this in a very disciplined way.[13]

A second paradox comes from the fact that, like several other Chinese entrepreneurs, Jack Ma thinks that all competitive advantages can only be temporary; they cannot be sustainable. But at the same time, he is obviously looking to create a sustainable company. He has publicly set the objective of having Alibaba survive until 2101. Why 2101? Because at 102 years of age, the company will have covered three different centuries since its creation in 1999. His approach differs from those American academic thinkers who, for decades, have been preaching about finding a sustainable competitive advantage. Jack Ma believes that, in an incredibly fast-moving and complex market like China, this is a useless exercise. What's important for him resides in a different kind of quest. His goal is beyond finding competitive advantages in a particular sector; rather, he seeks to constantly redefine the frontiers of the sector itself. The only way to survive is to always look for the optimal field of activity, to enter into new sectors, and even to invent them.

This is the way for Jack Ma to build a sustainable company with a great long-term future, even without being based on a clear, sustainable advantage.

This leads me to a third paradox. Jack Ma is persuaded that Alibaba's culture, which he wants to keep as Chinese as possible, is an asset for conquering other markets. He believes that a company cannot be competitive internationally without having a strong local culture. He often explains that you have to build on your nationality, then go beyond it—or better yet, transform the inherent qualities of your local culture into a strength that can help you conquer the world. Bernard Arnault does nothing less when he exports the French spirit through the houses of LVMH. And this is exactly what Zhang Ruimin also wants to achieve, turning Haier's company culture into a competitive asset.

U.S. In, China Out

Chinese business leaders today owe much to their predecessors who first paved the way and marked forever the young business history of their country. Back in the 1980s and 1990s, in a

Confucian, risk-adverse culture that revered authority and conformity, these pioneers dared to adopt capitalistic methods, a mere decade or two after the end of the Cultural Revolution. This required real courage because, at that time, people could be punished for taking capitalist initiatives. They had a real sense of risk; they were immersed in uncertainty. "They were crossing the river by feeling the stones,"[14] as Deng Xiaoping, China's leader during that period, would have said.

Today's new entrepreneurs, like Jack Ma, Robin Li, Ren Zhengfei, Lei Jun, Pony Ma, Li Shufu, Wang Jingbo, and Diane Wang, have all benefitted from this bold heritage. They form a generation of experimenters for whom change is the norm. They don't debate it, as is often done in the West. They live it and practice it naturally. This inclination for change is at the core of their DNA.

As with Japan in the sixties, China was initially a low-cost producer for Western industry. That still remains partly true today, thanks to the gigantic capacity of the country's millions of factories. Chinese companies have imposed the same disruptive approach upon their foreign competitors. They always try to offer products at a lower cost per unit. They squeeze production costs, reduce the cost of materials, and make goods with only the functions or features their buyers really need. At a later stage, and only once they have consolidated their position within a given market, will they start to upgrade their products.

This is how Huawei built its worldwide leadership position. Over the past two decades, the company has become the world's biggest manufacturer of telecom-network equipment, rivaled only by Ericsson and Cisco. Huawei started off just a little more than 20 years ago by becoming a provider for the poorer inland provinces in China. Then, step by step, Huawei spread out to the international market, initially targeting smaller businesses in the least prosperous countries. It found ways to develop versions of its products specially adapted to secondary-market players. It exported its Chinese business model—starting by the low end of the market, and then progressively upgrading—rather than taking the European and American competition head on. Then, steadily, it bridged the technological gap that separated itself from its western rivals, and finally became installed in the developed markets. And so, to quote Edward Tse, "Huawei has gradually transformed the world's telecom-equipment market into something resembling China."[15]

More recently, China has made remarkable progress in terms of technology. In a market where consumer demand for innovation is higher than anywhere, Chinese companies are increasingly at the forefront. In this country, entrepreneurs seem to have President Xi Jinping in mind. When asked what would be critical for the long-term future of China, he replied, "Innovation, innovation, innovation."[16] His voice was heard. China is now the world champion in new patents. In 2017 alone, they registered more new patents than the United States, South Korea, Japan, and Europe combined. Often unjustly accused of being a mere imitator, China is determined to overturn this stereotype.

More and more, Chinese companies are shaping entire sectors of the global economy, from mobile software to electronic devices, from health care to entertainment. As *Fast Company* put it, "With more than half of its 1.37 billion citizens online, 90 percent of them via smartphone, China has seen an explosion of tech behemoths and upstarts driving innovation hubs like Beijing and Shenzhen to become more hypercompetitive than even Silicon Valley."[17]

Size is obviously an asset. For the past two decades, China has been experiencing the benefits of this competitive advantage that the United States has enjoyed for over a century. Both countries are so vast that costs involved in developing and launching new products are practically amortized by the time they come to launch abroad. I've often observed how perilous it is for companies born in Europe to try to attack the American or Chinese markets. To succeed worldwide, to win in the United States and in China, they have to take more risks than companies coming from either of those countries. In any case, Chinese companies have already moved on to the next phase. According to Connie Chan, a partner at Andreessen Horowitz: "For any one company in the U.S., there might be 10 equivalents in China. In order to survive, you have to iterate that much faster."[18]

We have been witness to two contrasting periods. In the first, which I would describe as *U.S. in*, Chinese businessmen copied American business models, then transformed them to become more appropriate for Chinese needs. Time has moved on. In 2014, Haier's CEO told Edward Tse:

> In the past, the management of Chinese companies was really simple. All we had to do was learn from Japanese or American companies. But now, we have no example to reference, especially in the reform of large companies. [19]

The Chinese way of doing things is showing itself to be increasingly competitive on a worldwide basis. Chinese companies have traced their own paths. We have entered a new era, one of *China out*.

Chinese businesses no longer seek answers to the turbulent world we live in. Instead, they are looking to actually contribute to the turbulence. The Chinese compulsion to drive companies from one transformation to the next is unique. In the West, the drive for transformation is typically reserved for technology companies, start-ups, and small firms. In China it's true for everyone, even the most traditional of enterprises.

Jack Ma is the incarnation of this evolution. In the 1980s he devoured books on American management methods, in search of inspiration. But he maintained a certain critical distance toward them. He had this interesting phrase about the language he used to teach in school: "English helps me a lot. . . . It makes me understand the distance between China and the world."[20] His decades of experience help him understand the difference between Western imports that are useful and those that are not worthwhile. Perhaps unintentionally, he and his fellow Chinese CEOs have traced the outline of what could be called one day "the Chinese way." The world of American business has led the thinking of corporate leaders for the last half-century, but now it's quite possible that Chinese entrepreneurs will step into the spotlight. They will have a hand in rewriting the rules.

Much has been said about China's GDP having been the highest in the world at the end of the 18th century. Perhaps the trajectory of Chinese business is putting things back in their right place. Chinese chief executives share the dream of seeing their country reclaim its position as one of the world's greatest hubs for scientific ideas and technological advances. If not the greatest. But this goes way beyond merely contributing to China's renaissance. As creators of many of the fastest-growing enterprises in the world, they are aware of their huge potential influence. Chinese CEOs know that they are riding a historic wave of economic activity. They are changing the geopolitics of business.

The ambitions of Chinese chief executives are not lowly. "We don't want to be number one in China. We want to be number one in the world,"[21] Jack Ma once told the *South China Morning Post* newspaper. That was at the very beginning, when Alibaba company had fewer than 20 employees. Today, even if his company employs some 50,000 people, Jack Ma continues to strongly believe that the company's Chinese mind-set is the key to its success.

Meg Whitman, eBay's chief executive, learned this the hard way. After being forced to abandon the Chinese market, confronted with the ferocious resistance of Alibaba, she exclaimed one day, "Whoever wins China will win the world."[22]

PART
TWO

DISRUPTIVE
BUSINESS THINKING

I have often wondered how Chinese businessmen, now in their sixties and brought up outside the market economy, learned to run companies. How did they understand the business world? By devouring, as we've seen, American books. They knew how to transport academic thought into real life. Business literature opened the eyes of Zhang Ruimin and Jack Ma, whose parents had spent a lifetime ignoring everything related to free enterprise.

U.S. business literature is a discipline in itself, a subset of the social sciences, a specific area of thought from the country with the largest number of major companies in the world. Authors have forged central ideas. Concepts such as core competencies, quality circles, reengineering, portfolio management, value migration, sustainable competitive advantage, and also contingency planning, knowledge workers, the balanced scorecard, the value chain—the list is quite long. Their personal theories shed new light on what goes on in the world of business. They reveal new trends and allow readers to see companies' successes or failures through a new prism.

Among the best known of these authors are Peter Drucker, Gary Hamel, Michael Hammer, Charles Handy, Michael Porter, Tom Peters, and Jim Collins. I've met two of them, Gary Hamel and Tom Peters. Gary Hamel became world-famous when he published *Leading the Revolution* and he was the keynote speaker of a symposium on breakthrough strategies we organized with the Conference Board in 1992. The goal of this event was to launch our Disruption methodology. I have also met Tom Peters, the author of *In Search of Excellence*, several times. He has been a big supporter of our methodology, and even contributed to the cover of one of my books by being the first to say, "Disrupt or die."[1]

In this part, I talk about three business writers who are uncontestably disruptive thinkers. The first is Jim Collins, who led the world of business thinking from 1980 to 2000. One of his books, *Good to Great*, is still among the bestselling business books of all time. The second is Clayton Christensen, today's most famous Harvard professor, thanks to *The Innovator's Dilemma*, his work on the subject of disruptive innovation. The third is Jedidiah Yueh, a start-up entrepreneur who has a profound understanding of the digital world. Yueh's essay, *Disrupt or Die*[2], is very knowledgeable about what drives Silicon Valley's entrepreneurs. And he should know; he is one of them—and a very successful one at that.

CHAPTER 7

JIM COLLINS

ON THE SEARCH FOR EXCELLENCE AND THE MANAGEMENT OF ALTERNATIVES

J im Collins's books are full of common sense. Even if he collects masses of facts and data in his quest to define excellent companies, his work is never overly academic. It is quite empirical and provides readers with really useful inspiration.

The title of his bestseller *Good to Great*[1] gives a good clue as to its theme: how companies and individuals can strive to approach excellence. Millions of copies have been sold. Collins's first book, *Built to Last*, has also stood the test of time and one of its chapters has become particularly famous. That chapter deals with the difficulty of deciding between two options posed as alternatives. It's about what he calls the "Tyranny of the Or."[2]

The world has obviously changed a lot since Collins wrote these two books, but they both remain as relevant as ever. Collins's thinking has not aged.

Good to Great

Our Los Angeles agency, TBWA\Chiat\Day, is where Apple's great advertising campaigns have been born since we started working for Apple, in 1983. The agency's founder, Jay Chiat, used to love to say "Good enough is not enough."[3] This credo had such an impact that it has been progressively taken up by the entire TBWA organization. It may not seem like much, but referring to it constantly—whether while developing a strategy or imagining a campaign—makes it a constant challenge. In today's marketing world, where the motto is often "Cheap, fast, and good enough," this is especially true.

Chiat and Collins developed their signature mindsets at the end of the last century. You could say that the world has moved on since then. When Collins wrote his bestsellers, the word *disruption* had not yet made its way into the business lexicon. In fact, the popular theory of the day, the concept of constant quality improvement (CQI), contradicted the idea of rupturing with what came before.

At the time, Collins was already being criticized for underestimating the impact of the technological revolution and we were only at the very beginning of the Internet age. Despite this, in today's world of turbulence, volatility, and complexity, one of Collins's principles remains more valid than ever. It can be summarized as follows: The primary quality of a leader lies not just in strategic intelligence or management aptitude, but in the capacity to bring clarity. Without clarity, everything slows down, becomes eroded, and eventually dissipates. Clarity provides sense and points of reference.

According to Collins, great leaders clarify what is vital and what is less so. They are able to formulate this in such a way that the entire company becomes aligned. Jim Burke, one of Johnson and Johnson's great chief executives, devoted over a third of his time explaining to employees the company's credo and the consequences in their work. The same goes for Jack Ma, who is just as passionate about sharing knowledge now as he was at the start of his career, 25 years ago, when he was a teacher. He spends much of his time communicating what he believes in and telling how Alibaba has to constantly reinvent itself. He loves to say that, for him, CEO stands for chief education officer.

It is necessary to clarify the difference between what a company can potentially do better than any other and, equally important, what it cannot. For Collins, this is the first step on the path that brings companies from good to great. Collins says:

> It is not a goal to be the best, a strategy to be the best, an intention to be the best, a plan to be the best. It is an understanding of what you can be the best at. The distinction is absolutely crucial.[4]

The right words must be found to express what a company is best at. For this to be well said, it must be written down. At a recent TBWA Executive Committee meeting, Nancy Koehn, a professor at the Harvard Business School and at Omnicom University, underlined the importance of committing words to paper. The written words will eventually be spoken by people in the company and will create the essential cultural cement. She went as far as stating this paradox: "Writing helps you understand your own thoughts."[5]

A great way to bring clarity is to define the company's reason for being, to formulate its purpose. *Purpose* is not a new concept; Peter Drucker was talking about it back in the fifties. When a company gives itself an engaging and relevant purpose, it obtains a competitive advantage. Purpose is the reason for a company to exist, over and above just making money. The purpose must be written down and nurtured for years—even decades—to come. It's never fully realized, just as a horizon cannot be reached.

Some brands and companies have given great clarity to their purpose. Pampers, P&G's $10 billion brand, is not just about selling better-performing diapers and providing parents with better comfort for their babies. The purpose the brand has given itself is to "care for all babies' happy, healthy development, and for young mothers' welfare."[6] This has led the company to take a number of useful initiatives not just for babies, but also for pregnant women and those who have just given birth.

Dove is another example. Since its creation in 1955, the brand has claimed that it doesn't sell simple soap, but beauty bars. It has always embraced the concept of beauty. And 10 years ago, it worked to integrate the idea that there is beauty in everyone. Dove's purpose is to help women establish greater self-esteem. The brand says so itself, "We believe beauty should be a source of confidence, and not anxiety."[7]

Companies born in the digital era are no less ambitious. Airbnb wants us to discover a world where everyone can belong everywhere: a world with no strangers. This is a very worthwhile purpose.

Collins believes that, above all, a purpose should be profoundly sincere. For him, authenticity prevails over uniqueness. This is why he often uses examples of purpose that, at first sight, might appear somewhat simplistic, even banal. For instance, consider Disney's purpose, "make people happy,"[8] or Hewlett-Packard's "make technical contributions for the advancement and welfare of humanity."[9] Perhaps due to my advertising background, I always look for differentiation. I have a distinct preference for purposes with more specific substance, like those of Pampers, Dove, or Airbnb. These seem to me better equipped to fit Collins's objective of understanding and communicating what you can be the best at.

Collins directed his advice to companies, but it can also apply to individuals. I don't mean just the heads of industry, but also people who don't have management responsibilities, those who do not lead, but are led. They, too, can try to go from good to great. This is what William Faulkner suggested when he gave the advice: "Don't bother just to be better than your contemporaries or predecessors. Try to be better than yourself."[10]

The Era of the *And*

In 1994, Collins denounced the "Tyranny of the Or." He explained in his book *Built to Last* that posing a problem in terms of alternatives, A or B, reduces the scope of possibilities. It locks the thought process into conventional approaches, and reduces the ambition to stray from well-trodden paths. Alternatives often turn out to be too restrictive. They imperfectly describe issues in a world that is more and more complex, harder and harder to understand. Collins was one of the first to explain that we have entered the era of the *and*.

The capacity to reconcile opposing forces is a common trait among great captains of industry and it extends to all aspects of management. As we all know, business leaders are constantly faced with contradictory objectives. They have to reconcile the short and long terms, conjugate internal and external growth, and determine the point of equilibrium between global and local, between centralization and decentralization. When it comes to choosing employees, they must find a fair balance between internal promotion and outside hiring. They must manage the synergy between generalists and specialists, knowing that despite specialists' essential skills, it's often the broader experience of generalists that provides the alchemy at the heart of the creation of real value. They must also make the crucial decision of what should come from internal research and what should be brought by outside partners. Finally, they have to reconcile their shareholders' expectations of return on investment and their employees' no less legitimate demands for a fair reward.

Refusing to become trapped between two sets of alternatives preserves your mental agility. It allows you to integrate different points of view without settling for an often-sterile equilibrium. Instead of choosing by excluding things, leaders should make decisions by reconciling contraries. Francis Scott Fitzgerald wrote on this: "The test of a first-rate intelligence is the ability to hold two opposed ideas in the mind at the same time, and still retain the ability to function."[11]

Steve Jobs did not choose between software and hardware, but brought them together into each of his devices, with the one allowing Apple to charge a premium for the other. Bernard Arnault did not choose between making LVMH's brands more and more prestigious or making luxury accessible to all. He did both at the same time. As for Herb Kelleher, he did not sacrifice quality for low cost at Southwest Airlines.

But with time, I have learned that it is not always possible to reconcile the two alternatives in an either/or choice. The answer does not necessarily reside in the *both* option, but it can be somewhere else—in a third place.

Toyota decided to hold off on making electric cars until the market was ready and public authorities had installed the necessary charging infrastructure. But Toyota could not ignore the essential place that electricity would play in the future. So, the Japanese company opted for a third way, the hybrid car.

Space X's technology is another example. When starting Space X, Elon Musk faced a difficult choice. On the one hand, he could attempt to raise massive funds to finance a program that would have been as expensive as that of Arianespace, which completed 11 launches in 2018. On the other hand, Musk could settle for a program that has less frequent launches. The solution lay elsewhere and it seemed natural once it was found. It was to employ reusable booster engines. These were more expensive to make initially, but could be reused up to once a week. As a result, they could be amortized quickly enough to render Elon Musk's intended business model viable.

What is true for business also goes for the world of nonprofit. I work for UNICEF. Like many people, I was shocked to learn of the conditions suffered in the United States by migrants' children. France is also far from exemplary when it comes to the treatment of migrants. In this country, children continue to be interned with their parents in detention centers. Many think the only two solutions are to separate children from their parents or to lock the families up together. However, there is a third option. We looked for it, and found it being used in Ireland and some Nordic countries. Immigrants there are not confined in detention centers. Instead, they simply have to register themselves and their children every week at the closest police station. If they fail to do so, they are immediately kicked out of the country. This proves that the choice of separating children or keeping families incarcerated is a false choice.

I've cited these different examples to underline the fact that, when confronted with a choice between two unsatisfactory alternatives, it's often productive to look for the solution elsewhere. In order not to allow yourself to become trapped in, it's worth searching for a third option.

A last point: When one observes such contradictory forces, it appears that they are often expressed in the form of a paradox. The *Harvard Business Review* went as far as to talk about the importance of knowing how to "unleash the power of paradox."[12]

According to the article, a primary quality of great leaders is the capability to thrive on paradoxes and use them to discover original solutions.

Here are some examples of paradoxes:

"It's still the L'Oreal of always, but has nothing to do with the L'Oreal of yesterday,"[13] *Jean-Paul Agon, chairman and CEO of L'Oreal.*

"Our task is to read things that are not yet on the page,"[14] *Steve Jobs.*

"Finance is the only way to make money when you have no idea how to create wealth,"[15] *Peter Thiel, founder of PayPal.*

"I was so much older then. I'm younger than that now,"[16] *Bob Dylan.* *

It is worth dwelling on paradoxes. They always contain a hidden truth. A paradox with a seductive formulation prompts the thought process and leads us to question our own logic. Paradoxes are the spark between two contradictory ideas. The apparent contradiction in terms obliges us to reflect, works on us from the inside, and liberates us from conventional thinking.

Niels Bohr, co-founder of the quantum theory of physics, summed it up beautifully: "How wonderful that we have met with a paradox. Now we have some hope of making progress."[17]

CHAPTER 8

CLAYTON CHRISTENSEN

ON DISRUPTIVE INNOVATION

While Jim Collins thinks in terms of paradox, Clayton Christensen does so in terms of dilemma. But when it comes to analyzing the conflicting objectives faced by heads of industry, both are in agreement. In his bestseller *The Innovators' Dilemma*,[1] Christensen examines two alternatives. Should a company prioritize protecting its existing business, or investing more massively to counter disruptive innovators, who, sooner or later, will drastically alter the market? This choice is all the more difficult since, most often, radical innovations provoke a change in a company's economic model. Christensen's alternatives are at the heart of the eternal debate between improvement and transformation, exploitation versus exploration.

In *The Innovator's Dilemma*, Christensen introduces the notion of "disruptive innovation," the concept that made him famous. He first described the idea 24 years ago in the *Harvard*

Business Review[2] and, since then, it has been subject to analysis the world over. The concept describes how companies enter the market at the low end, build a solid base of consumers, then move progressively upmarket, destabilizing or even annihilating existing companies that have been present in their market sector for decades.

This theory owes its success to the original thinking of its author, but also, and this is far from negligible, to his judicious choice to use the expression "disruptive innovation." The distinction between gradual innovations and non-gradual ones had been established for decades. In 1962, Thomas Kuhn introduced the idea of "discontinuity."[3] Then in the late seventies, academics and business analysts referred to "discontinuous innovation." Christensen's term, "disruptive innovation," sounds better. It's memorable. It has contributed largely to spreading his theory.

In semantic terms, the path had already been cleared for him. He coined the expression "disruptive innovation" years after our agency had launched the Disruption methodology.[4] Our initial work on disruption in the early nineties had already begun to popularize the expression. Christensen started to use the adjective *disruptive*, whose connotation is less entrenched than the noun *disruption*. Over the years, journalists and writers began using simply the word *disruption* to qualify Christensen's thinking. The Harvard professor even ended up adopting the word himself.

Christensen is indeed a disruptive thinker and he has left his mark on the academic world as no one else has over the past 20 years. The books he has published, and the articles that they prompted, have stimulated massive discussion of the word *disruption* and provoked a lasting wave of reactions.

His theory has proved itself clearly useful. Christensen uses his model to show how many companies were disrupted and how he can alert others to the nature of the dangers that may threaten them.

Yet, as I will explain later in this chapter, this concept, like all theories, is constrained by its proper limits. I recommend not to applying it systematically, but rather learning to use it the right way, with discernment. Above all, this allows me to emphasize a point that is very important to me, namely that *disruption* does not always equate with *destruction*. Far from it. Christensen's thinking has kept this debate alive.

Bottom-up Disruption

In trying to continually improve their offers, many companies eventually end up producing products and services that are actually too sophisticated, too expensive, and too complicated. In doing so, these companies create space at the bottom of the market for the entry of those companies Christensen identifies as "disruptive innovators." The entrants that seize this opportunity begin by giving a new population of customers access to a product category at the low end. Later, they progressively move upmarket and conquer a share of the historical consumer base belonging to legacy companies, thus upheaving those established positions, sometimes to the point of disruption.

Salesforce is frequently used as an example to illustrate the theory of disruptive innovation. This is because its chief executive officer, Marc Benioff, initially targeted small companies and start-ups, to whom he offered his software on a free trial basis. At that time, Salesforce's software was much simpler and less sophisticated than what was being proposed by its competitors. Benioff gradually added new functions, enabling Salesforce to move upmarket and, in doing so, permanently destabilize Siebel, which was the market leader at the time.

Huawei is another example. As we've already discussed, the Chinese company started by conquering the low end of its domestic market before little by little enriching its offer. When the time came to turn to foreign markets, you might have thought that Huawei would have exported the improved versions of its products, which were better suited to Western needs. This was not the case. Instead, Huawei opted for an inverse strategy, first exporting its low-end products worldwide. This is how it imposed its business model, country by country. Huawei's approach reflects Christensen's theory. Only after penetrating markets at the bottom end did Huawei begin to upgrade its offer.

The originality of Christensen's thinking resides in this double movement: the entry by the low-end, then the progression up the value chain toward the top. At the beginning, the offer is less expensive and simpler. It democratizes innovation by being accessible to most. It's what Ford's Model T did 100 years ago, and more recently Club Med or Ikea. Today, most start-ups provide access to new markets. They tend to penetrate at the bottom, and then create a new kind of consumption or usage. Christensen had thus defined the principles that would guide the success of future start-ups, 10 years before they even existed. Recognizing this pattern, he was also able to predict the fate of Kodak long before its fall.

Christensen's theory was rightly credited with having a real ability to predict. It helped existing, established companies be alert and be prepared. The bottom-up disruption sequence he describes exposes the potential risks these companies will be confronted with. This highlights a dilemma, and also a paradox. According to the Harvard professor, if companies fail, it's not because their managers made bad decisions, but rather because they continued to follow the same logic and apply the same decisions that had previously made them successful. Success, which induces a kind of blindness, prevents them from seeing growing menaces. "Doing the right thing turns out to be the wrong thing to do,"[5] as Christensen wrote.

The Disruption Controversy

All this being said, no conceptual framework, however irrefutable it may appear, can avoid attracting a degree of controversy. When cases no longer fit into its established model, a theory can become contested.

Jill Lepore, a fellow professor of Christensen's at Harvard, published an article in the *New Yorker* magazine[6] that created considerable media noise by attempting to deconstruct Christensen's theory. She points out that many of the companies that he qualifies as failures actually ended up being successful.

Two other professors of the Sloan Business School at MIT have since written another critical paper. After close examination of 77 of the examples[7] of disruptive innovation Christensen cites in his books *The Innovator's Dilemma* and *The Innovator's Solution*, they argue that his hypotheses should be taken with caution. Both MIT scholars come to the conclusion that predictions based on Christensen's theory do not always prove true.

As a result, Christensen has sometimes struggled with his own model in order to preserve it—and he has used it to issue some questionable predictions. For instance, in 2007 he projected the failure of the iPhone. More recently, he claimed that there was nothing disruptive about Uber. This latter assertion led me to publish an article in *Forbes*,[8] explaining that some of Christensen's conclusions are open to question. For me, Uber is a real disruption, but one which does not fit into the professor's established framework. Using his definition, the majority of recent well-known success stories, including Xiaomi, Alibaba, Big Bazaar, Tesla, and Whole Foods, are not real disruptions. The same goes for Apple. The greatest disruptor of the past 20 years never entered the market at the bottom. On the contrary, the iMac, iPod, and iPad positioned themselves at the top of the market from the outset. This is the risk most theories have to face, however brilliant and solid they may seem. They end up having to force-fit the facts into a predetermined framework.

In my view, Christensen's theory has two notable shortcomings. First of all, it does not help to resolve the famous dilemma at the origin of his first book. On the one hand, companies need to protect existing revenue streams, which are essential to their short-term success but, on the other hand, they must support new activities that will be vital to their future. How must organizations manage these competing priorities? How should they allocate resources? Christensen sheds no light on these answers and, yet, the decision is crucial.

Second, and contrary to what the theory implies, disruption does not equal destruction—at least not systematically. It's true that many business commentators tend to agree with Christensen that all disruptive innovations finish by upheaving markets, and thus definitively destabilizing the established order. Put otherwise, they are revealed as being resolutely destructive. However, for me, this point of view is restricting. It ignores an entire field of innovation, the one perhaps most relevant for legacy companies: that of non-destructive disruptive innovations.

There are a great many examples of such cases, including Nespresso, Club Med, Ikea, Southwest Airlines, Haier, Toms, Starbucks, Marriott, and Visa. These and a lot of other companies have profoundly innovated without ever having been destructive along the way.

Many business leaders, consciously or not, may have been too influenced by Christensen's work to recognize this. They have accepted the idea that disruption necessarily leads to destruction, and this impacts how they see innovation. They thus deprive themselves of a great number of opportunities. Disruption can help businesses gain sizeable market share, without destroying the market.

Not all companies are obliged to be Uber or Airbnb.

CHAPTER 9

JEDIDIAH YUEH

ON THE BEHAVIORS OF COMPANIES OF THE NEW ECONOMY

The *Wall Street Journal* ran in 2016 an article entitled, "The Economy's Hidden Problem: We're Out of Big Ideas."[1] How can a journalist pose such a stark assertion when we all feel we are living in a world full of innovation?

The preeminence of Apple, Facebook, Google, and Amazon; the breakthrough of nanotechnology and biotechnology; the start-up boom; and the growing power of artificial intelligence and virtual reality give us the impression that innovation is omnipresent. And yet, technology industries and others born of the Internet represent only a fraction of the economy. They will encompass much more in the future, but until then, the companies of the new economy cannot compensate for the insufficient rate of innovation of the other so-called traditional companies.

This is the case for companies in many sectors such as food, cosmetics, pharmaceuticals, banking, and insurance.

American statistics show that in the past 10 years the rhythm of innovation in these kinds of companies is greatly inferior to that of the previous 10 years. It may seem counterintuitive but, according to an MIT estimate, research productivity in the United States has dropped by an average of 5.3 percent[2] per year over the past 10 years. The "Vitality Index," which is the percentage of total revenues generated by new products and services, is in net decline in the quasi-totality of sectors. The return on investment coming from research and development is nothing compared to what it was 20 or 30 years ago. A partner at Accenture concludes unambiguously that corporate innovation has become sterile.

Why this decline? I see several reasons. First, when companies excel in what they do, it takes longer for them to detect their loss of creativity. Research investment is directed toward improving companies' current strengths rather than discovering something new. The role of R&D focuses more on protecting existing market share than on expanding the market. The second explanation, I believe, is that companies do not work through the dilemma described by Christensen (see Chapter 8). The strategic allocation of resources between incremental and disruptive innovations has not been clearly defined. Currently, incremental innovation is more prevalent than disruptive innovation. Third, the decline in creativity happens in many companies that have prioritized cost cutting. The all-powerful purchasing department is hardly a guarantee of openness to new ideas. Finally, many companies find themselves locked into old habits, methods, and procedures, trapping themselves in a conventional way of doing things. They do not innovate in the way they innovate.

In 2015, these observations led me to write a book encouraging companies to look for new sources of inspiration, to open themselves up, and to not be satisfied with incremental innovation alone. Titled *The Ways to New*[3], the book described different types of innovation such as asset-based innovation, reverse innovation, revival-based innovation, data-driven innovation, usage-based innovation, and price-led innovation, to mention just a few. Fifteen different paths to innovation were proposed. Of the many companies I've known, very few ever follow more than two or three.

Then, I also turned my attention to start-ups. A great many traditional companies have partnered with or acquired some of them, hoping to increase their own capacity to innovate. Specialist investment funds, incubators, technopoles, and accelerators are appearing everywhere but cultural differences make these partnerships difficult, sometimes even hazardous. Not many new ideas are emerging from these innovation platforms, think tanks, and labs. If they were, the statistics on R&D productivity would be different.

I looked more closely at start-ups to see how they could inspire established companies and I ran up against a well-known fact. For each successful start-up, there are hundreds that fail. This tiny percentage is explained by the fact that success depends on so many different external factors that are difficult to foresee. Luck is a very random element of success, so it appeared perilous to try to establish serious conclusions on the way start-ups function— until I read Jedidiah Yueh's book *Disrupt or Die: What the World Needs to Learn from Silicon Valley to Survive the Digital Era.*

Founding CEO of Avamar, which pioneered the data deduplication market, Yueh is now the chief executive officer of Delphix, a dynamic data platform provider. In his book, Yueh describes operating systems and Internet protocols, and explains how, today, "products are designed for software as the end user."[4] And over and above these purely technical aspects, he also gives real insights into how start-ups work.

I have combined Yueh's thoughts with those of Peter Thiel, author of *Zero to One*, and Eric Ries, author of *Lean Startup*. My conversations with other founders of start-ups have also influenced my thinking. Getting such diverse opinions has allowed me to develop a list of lessons about the new-economy operators that I believe could be interesting for old-economy businesses too.

I have pooled these thoughts together under seven different themes. They are very diverse, even disparate, and each should be looked at on its own. There is no particular connection between them, except my belief that they can be helpful to all kinds of companies.

Lessons from an Entrepreneur

1. "Don't be dispirited by the magnitude of complexity ahead,"[5] counsels Yueh.

   He demystifies, at least in part, the fantastic innovations coming out of Silicon Valley. The ideas behind Instagram, LinkedIn, Uber, or Airbnb are not that far from being some-what "mundane," to use his own word. Even Google, as he explains, was created from a simple observation:

   > In the world of academia, published papers are often judged by their citations, how often they are cited, and the importance of each citation. Two PhD students decided to apply that concept to counting and weighing the value of links on websites (instead of citations)—an automated way to rank search results. Google is born.[6]

Of course, this has required highly qualified engineers to conceive and constantly upgrade the algorithms that make Google the leader of Internet search. In the past, Internet companies had to develop their own proprietary information technologies, but today anybody can buy limitless infrastructure and software to scale across a huge number of servers. The core infrastructures that allowed Amazon and Google to come into existence are now mere commodities, often available as a service, or even for free.

I would say that the essential point lies elsewhere. I have distinguished what I believe are four major sources of inspiration for starting a new business. An entrepreneur needs to discover one of the following:

- An unanswered need
- A residual point of friction
- A market gap not filled
- An insight not yet identified

It can be very productive to clearly differentiate between these four possible springboards. They are not simply alternative ways of talking about the same thing. They are each really different.

Once you have identified one of these springboards, you must advance step by step, stage by stage, and not allow yourself to become submerged by the technology.

2. There is no start-up with a slow culture.

For start-ups, speed is everything. They seek to develop and grow while knowing they have an infinitesimal chance of surviving. In any case, to have the slightest chance, they have to be faster than the competition.

In California, many start-ups practice weekly planning. They separate the budget cycle from the rhythm of their company's business life. The acceleration of time frames makes annual planning counterproductive. They prefer to start each new week with three questions that each workshop, department, or service asks itself:

- What did we do right last week?
- What is the objective for this week?
- What do we need to reach this objective?

Some go as far as giving themselves the day as a unit of time. This may be natural for developers, who are looking to build solutions in real time, but it is also the case in some very big Chinese enterprises—for example Haier and Alibaba—where workers see themselves given daily objectives. Objectives are defined in the morning and the output is evaluated against them at the end of the same day.

Silicon Valley start-ups that behave this way think the slowness with which legacy companies operate will be their downfall. Whatever the sector, traditional companies would be well advised to speed up their rhythm to allow themselves to make decisions more swiftly and to accelerate their rate of innovation. Speed is the very first thing traditional companies should copy from start-ups.

3. You cannot conceive of a disruptive strategy or action plan without "playing offense."[7]

Yueh cites Predix, the industrial platform of GE as a counter example. Jeff Immelt, the former CEO, declared that he wanted to build "the world's largest industrial Internet of Things."[8] Four years later, success has been mixed, to such an extent that GE is talking of selling Predix. There are scientific and business reasons for this, but organizational ones as well. Management was unable to convince other GE divisions to adopt the Predix platform, which is obviously the worst possible message you could send to potential clients. A large, heavy division, Predix was bogged down in GE bureaucracy—a very different scenario from the nimble ways of operating of other software companies. Yueh sees this as the primary explanation of what ended as a setback for GE. However good your digital transformation program may be, you can't expect to move an industrial company into the top 10 software companies in just a few years without deeply restructuring—without being truly on the offensive.

Yueh sees this as the primary explanation of what ended as a setback for GE. However good your digital transformation program may be, you can't expect to move an industrial company into the top 10 software companies in just a few years without being truly on the offensive.

My own take on this is threefold.

First, digital transformation is often seen as a period of transition: difficult and painful, but limited in time. I believe that the opposite is true: Companies have to accept that transformation will be perpetual. In order to succeed, they will have to follow successive, never-ending steps.

This leads us to the second point: To consider that any organizational system will only be provisional. Few companies force themselves to regularly question the way they operate. The reality is that any organization must be sufficiently fluid if it wants to succeed in periodic transformation. In Chapter 5, I discussed Zhang Ruimin, CEO of Haier, who has on several occasions shaken up his organization from top to bottom. Recently, he transformed it into a kind of platform, containing thousands of independently managed units. Every time Zhang is questioned on the reasons behind the success of Haier, he gives the regular transformations of his company's structure as the main one.

Finally, I would add that evolving an organization is not an end in itself but rather a means, a lever to render the company more innovative. I have already referred to the fact that most traditional companies have an innovation deficit and that, willingly or not, they tend to lean toward incremental, rather than disruptive, innovation. By contrast, start-ups and the most innovative traditional businesses demonstrate the point to which organizational models can be the catalysts for all kinds of innovation.

To reiterate, many companies engaged in digital transformation are just looking for incremental improvement. And this is where Yueh's thinking is crucial. He believes companies should embark upon radical change and look for disruptive organizational models.

4. Whatever the product or service you're offering, it may be useful to consider if part of it can or should be offered for free.

Knowing how to distinguish between "users and buyers"[9] is a key element for Yueh. Users of Google pay nothing; only the advertisers, the buyers, are invoiced for the services they receive. The ultimate aim is to make free services even more valuable than those that are paid for. To expand on this point of view, I suggest that companies think seriously about what they could, or should, make free.

Spotify is an interesting example. This company offers free access to the world's biggest music catalogue; however, it limits this access, in the hope of turning new listeners into paid subscribers. Free listening time is capped at 10 hours per month. No piece of music can be heard more than five times. You might think such constraints would put customers off. They do, but the offer is so attractive that users become hooked and cannot bring themselves to forego paying the subscription.

Giving things away for free should not be left to only Internet companies. I recently asked the chief executive officers of two major worldwide legacy companies, "What if you decided to offer part of your products and services for free?" This is one of the questions about innovation that we always ask our clients during Disruption Days. We propose a list of questions which might not seem obvious.

The question I posed to these two CEOs intrigued them. It caused them to reflect. I believe that provocative "what if" questions can prompt thinking that ends up improving business models, and sometimes even imagining new ones. In this case, a free offer can be a lever for growth for a traditional company, as it often is for an Internet pure player.

5. Data is the best tool for legacy companies to "maintain their positions in the face of digital disruptors,"[10] underlines Yueh.

Because they were born on the web, agents of the Internet economy benefit from an advantage over traditional, legacy companies. The giants, Google, eBay, LinkedIn, Facebook, or the tens of thousands of start-ups created every year are built around big data since the outset. It's their natural habitat, in which they've always evolved. They didn't have to reconcile or merge big data technology with their current IT infrastructures, unlike legacy companies.

By contrast, legacy companies actually have a determining advantage. Unlike new market entrants, they have the resources and financial means to invest massively in such things as hardware platforms, databases, extraction software, advanced analytic tools, maintenance, and storage systems. However, legacy companies, in their permanent state of anxiety about digital disruptors, have often forgotten that they have the means to prevail. If they accelerate their speed to keep pace with the digital economy, they can become the real key players of the upcoming "analytics 3.0" era.

The challenge they face is how to make sense of all the new streams of data that they have collected from a variety of different sources. This data, which can be structured or unstructured, internal or external, is, for the most part, disconnected. Companies need to learn how to exploit this richness by changing the way they operate internally and ensuring that the way they work fits with the new technology available. They need *translators* to incorporate big data into their business strategy in an understandable way, to bridge the data gap between CMOs and CIOs and help them to work closely together. Equally importantly, they must clarify what data matters most for them, which is, in fact, the most challenging task they have.

According to Cisco and McKinsey, "By 2020, some 50 billion smart devices will be connected, along with billions of smart sensors."[11] Connected devices will generate an unprecedented diversity and volume of information in real time. For companies, this data will become assets as vital as proprietary technologies or financial resources. Companies will need to give themselves the means to exploit this abundance of information, most of which is currently unexploited. McKinsey states, "Though about 90 percent of the digital data ever created in the world has been generated in just the past two years, only 1 percent of the data has been analyzed."[12]

6. David Packard, a founder of Hewlett-Packard, once said, "No company can grow revenues consistently faster than its ability to get enough of the right people to implement that growth and still become a great company."[13]

Yueh saw the importance of this often-ignored advice primarily in his first company, Avamar. Located in Orange

County in Southern California, Avamar had difficulty hiring experienced executives and qualified engineers locally. And as a result, his company's growth was slower than he had hoped and, when Yueh sold it, it was undervalued. To avoid a similar outcome, he decided to base his second company, Delphix, where the talent was, in the heart of Silicon Valley.

Yueh describes this is in an unusual way. He explains that there is a parallel between how apps are developed and the geographical reality of Silicon Valley. The development for a basic app system starts off with the hardware platform, then the software platform, then the database, and finally, the front-end app. He had discovered that the Silicon Valley's geography mirrors the steps in basic app development, following the same four strata. In the south are located Apple, Intel, and Cisco. Moving north, one encounters Google and Facebook. Then, going further still, between San José and San Francisco, are companies like Oracle. Finally, at the northernmost point, in San Francisco, Uber, Airbnb, and Twitter are based. To be closest to the talent his business needed, he decided to install Delphix in Palo Alto, just between Oracle and the software companies.

This story highlights an unavoidable truth. It has become crucial to eliminate any barriers to the best talent. To attract the most competent staff around the world, a number of companies such as BMW, Siemens, Pfizer, DuPont, and L'Oreal are opening R&D centers in places where they can find the best engineers, computer technicians, or biologists. More and more frequently, Western companies find that their labs located in Shanghai, Seoul, or Tel Aviv are among their most productive. The center of gravity of innovation is shifting. Whatever the sector, whatever the company, executives increasingly understand that if they can't get the talent to move to them, they need to move to the talent.

7. In the start-up world, people are more open to changing their minds.

Yueh believes this to be an essential key to success in a digital world where time cycles are moving faster and faster. When time becomes the enemy, you cannot hang on too long to a bad idea. Tim Cook, Apple's CEO, says that Steve Jobs could completely change his mind from one day to the next. Yueh puts it paradoxically, "If they want to be 'right a lot,' leaders have to be willing to revise their understanding and reconsider what they already know." He concludes, "Leaders can't be obsessed with only one point of view."[14]

This is not dissimilar to Charles Darwin's philosophy as described by Charlie Munger, Warren Buffet's business partner. In his book, Yueh recalls the comparison drawn by Munger: "He [Darwin] tried to disconfirm his ideas as soon as he got them. He quickly put down in his notebook anything that disconfirmed a much-loved idea."[15]

These seven preceding points cover the views I have forged since reading the words of Yueh, Ries, and Peter Thiel, and also following discussions with the heads of many start-ups. I think that so-called conventional companies, which were not born from the Internet, can learn from these findings and apply them to their own ways of working, thus reinforcing their competitive stance.

Considering what Yueh writes in the conclusion of his book, this is more important than ever now, when established companies are being challenged more drastically than before. Yueh writes, "As the Innovation Cycle continues to accelerate, every company is about to be eaten by a software company. Even the software companies."[16] I cannot say if his predictions will come true, but I do know of a great many legacy companies from the old economy that I believe will be able to resist longer than Yueh thinks. Better than resist, they will know how to really take advantage of what this new world has to offer them.

The future is not yet written, and the old economy may still have a few surprises for us. It won't be the old economy versus the new economy but, as Jim Collins would have said, it will be both.

Category of One

Great entrepreneurs don't try to gain market share; they create markets. They branch out and create their own categories. They come up with totally different value propositions. They think beyond mere products, considering instead business models, as Apple, eBay, or Netflix have done so brilliantly. Companies that are neither technological nor digital, such as Starbucks, Lego, or Disney, have also succeeded in making such leaps. All of these organizations address customer needs that were previously unknown. They are not category leaders, but category creators, like Salesforce, which built the success of software as a service (SaaS).

In a 2011 *Harvard Business Review* issue, it was underlined that "Wall Street exponentially rewarded the category-creation companies, giving them $5.60 in incremental market capitalization for every $1.00 in revenue growth."[17] I imagine this is still the case today.

Thiel, who created PayPal, is also one of the associates of the Founders' Fund and was among the first to have invested in Facebook. His voice is one of the most listened-to in Silicon Valley. Thiel recommends creating monopolies. Considering that competition destroys profit margins, he incites people to create value where it is least expected. As a result, a monopolistic situation will emerge. In this way he denounces the "ideology of competition."[18] His thinking is based on common sense: "Every business is successful exactly to the extent that it does something others cannot."[19] So when he encourages young entrepreneurs to create their own monopolies, he's obviously not talking about illegal, but creative ones.

He gives lots of advice on the subject in his book *From Zero to One*. Here is some of it:

> "Creating value is not enough. You also need to capture some of the value you create."
>
> "If you've invented something new but you haven't invented an effective way to sell it, you have a bad business. No matter how good the product."
>
> "All companies must be 'lean,' which is code for 'unplanned.' Planning is arrogant and inflexible."
>
> "Selling your company to the media is a necessary part of selling it to everyone else."
>
> "Successful people find value in unexpected places."[20]

These points of view may first have been directed toward tech start-ups, but they can also be a source of inspiration for the heads of more traditional companies. Even today, the majority of new businesses created are not start-ups, in the strict sense of the word.

As for me, I advise clients looking for new sources of inspiration to proceed in the following way. Start with the four components of the digital revolution: sharing, disintermediation, transparency, and client centricity. It is always worthwhile for a company to ask how it can move to the next level on each of these topics. For instance, how could *sharing* take a different form than just crowdsourcing? What kinds of *disintermediation* can be envisaged? How can a company have more *transparency* in its activities? What is the difference between a company that says it's *customer-centric* and one that really gives the power to the consumer? These questions are at the very heart of a company's digital transformation and the answers can help it accelerate the rhythm of its innovations.

A major leader in the food industry, dominant in its market and apparently unattackable, asked us recently to imagine a competitive business model, one that would be highly destabilizing. We examined the company's current activities against the four components just described, and came back with some very competitive ideas. The result was particularly telling. The company in question has eventually integrated elements of the model we imagined, to better prepare itself against the entry of a disruptive newcomer into its sector. Of course, we will never know, but perhaps we have kept at bay, or discouraged, potential new entrants who were contemplating disrupting our client's business.

As this illustrates, innovation includes knowing in advance how to reduce the capacity of disruption by new competitors. If you cannot predict the future, at least you can always be prepared.

As General Douglas MacArthur once said, "The history of failure in war can almost be summed up in two words: too late."[21]

PART
THREE

DISRUPTIVE CORPORATE CULTURE

In this part, I don't refer to the word *culture* in its noble sense, literary, artistic, or scientific. I also don't mean it as *popular culture*, born of social networks and used daily by marketing and advertising agencies striving to insert their clients' brands into our lives.

What I want to evoke here is *corporate culture*. Definitions abound. Here are several that work harmoniously:

- "Culture is a blend of the values, beliefs, taboos, symbols, rituals, and myths companies develop over time."[1]
- "Culture is the tacit social order of an organization."[2]

- "Culture is the identity of a company as perceived by its best customers."[3]

To these brief definitions, I would add an extract from an article I wrote some years ago:

All corporate culture is the fruit of a collective adventure. The sensitivity and intelligence of thousands of men and women creating something they share in common. A mental structure, a communion of desires, a sort of collective élan. An interpretation of the future, coming from the values of the past.[4]

Corporate culture is evidently intangible. At first sight, it would appear to have nothing to do with the numbers. It's conceptual and unquantifiable; however, it can provide a real competitive advantage. As well as elements such as assets, turnover, growth, return on investment, share price, which are measurable, there also exist numerous studies that have *scientifically* proven the importance of a strong culture. The benefits of corporate culture are not just intuitive; they have been confirmed by the social sciences. James Heskett, who co-authored a book on the subject with John Kotter, analyzed the cultures of 200 companies and demonstrated the impact of culture on their results. He concluded, "On average, culture can account for 20 to 30 percent of the differential in performance when compared with the quartile which is the least culturally remarkable."[5]

On this subject, I often quote David Maister, former professor at Harvard Business School and member of Omnicom University. Over the course of his career, he has examined hundreds of service companies and questioned literally thousands of people. The data he gathered shines light on the direct correlation between culture and profit. Maister explains, "Offices with strong corporate cultures enjoy the highest employee satisfaction, and offices with the highest employee satisfaction are the most profitable ones."[6] In other terms, a powerful corporate culture attracts the best talent and contributes to employees' well-being. This, in turn, translates into increased productivity and reduced staff turnover, the combination of which goes on to generate higher profits and greater success.

Some may say that these facts are out of date, that the research is 20 years old, and that business has since moved on. These naysayers claim that giving too much credit to an old culture can be inhibiting. They see in it a desire to hide behind old-fashioned values, to be comforted by familiar behavior. For them, the notion of corporate culture is obsolete at best, a handicap at worst. They think that new-economy companies, where speed is of the essence, cannot be burdened with such a long-term concept.

I do not agree. For me, a strong corporate culture remains an essential asset, an incomparable element of cohesion, an indispensable cement that holds together a company's foundation. In my view, ultimately, the absence of a strong culture becomes a handicap.

The founders of Google and Netflix no doubt share this opinion. They have given their businesses distinct cultures that are consistently and actively references. This approach helps each company, in its own way, attract the best of the best. This is why I chose to dedicate the next two chapters to Google and Netflix, two companies that are living proof that corporate culture is as vitally important in new-economy companies.

I conclude this part with a few words on a culture that I know well, that of my company, TBWA. We are not, strictly speaking, a new-economy enterprise, yet our culture must remain totally in sync with popular culture. An agency must sense its time.

CHAPTER 10

SERGEY BRIN AND LARRY PAGE

ON RECRUITMENT POLICIES AND CORE VALUES

During the first half of the 20th century, people talked of "house style," "*esprit maison*" in French, as a way to describe the spirit that leaders of corporations wanted to infuse in their companies. Today this somewhat paternalistic concept seems a little old-fashioned. And yet in many ways, corporate culture is house style's heir. It has become a formidable weapon for all companies, including the most recent—and Google is no exception.

Google's culture first reveals itself in its employee benefits. The list is indeed impressive: free meals; massage treatments, medical and dental care at work; onsite gym, swimming pool, personal training, and yoga; company hairdressers; dry cleaners, and car wash; incentives on hybrid car purchases; extended maternity leave; life insurance; and so on. All of this has obviously contributed to creating a laid-back atmosphere and an employee-friendly environment. But make no mistake, this is not just about being kind. If Google is looking for ways to boost employees' well-being, it is doing so as a way to increase their productivity.

Company perks, the wide range of services provided to employees on site, save them precious time, which can then be redirected toward their work. People stay focused on their jobs. And they can fully enjoy their social lives without eating into their work time.

But at the same time, Google's culture obviously goes much further than these staff privileges. It also includes many timeless elements, fundamentals that constitute the basis for great corporate cultures and that have, over the decades, become constants. This is why Google is both old school and new. And it can inspire companies of the old economy as much as those of the new.

HR as a Science

Larry Page once said, "Google is not a conventional company. We do not intend to become one."[1] Avoiding becoming banal is an obsession.

It starts with the people the company recruits. Every year, Google receives around three million job applications, of which only 0.2 percent are hired. To filter and find the best, to recruit tailor-made candidates matching its culture, the company has developed a new approach to recruitment, one that is so particular that it has become famous. It is common knowledge that the questions candidates are subjected to are tough and unnerving. They have even inspired a bestseller called *Are You Smart Enough to Work at Google?* The company only wants to hire the brightest of the bright.

On the one hand, Google obviously is looking for very specific skills linked to the nature of its business. Most of Google's jobs require computing and coding capabilities. But at the same time, it is also looking for specific traits of character. They are not necessarily those you might expect to find in such a company; for instance, humility. Google means intellectual humility. As Laszlo Bock, former senior vice president of People Operations told *The New York Times*, it requires humility to step back and embrace the better ideas of others. "Without humility, you are unable to learn."[2]

The proportion of people hired without university degrees at Google has increased over time. Laszlo Bock has always been in favor of this, "When you look at people who don't go to school and make their way in the world, those are exceptional human beings. And we should do everything we can to find those people."[3]

New recruits feel privileged to have been chosen. Once they've joined Google, after having traversed all the testing steps they've been subjected to, everything is done to make them feel at home and to build their self-confidence. To prove the point, this is one comment from a mentor to a young employee, "Don't be afraid to ask questions—you don't have to impress me. You already have, and that's why I hired you."[4]

Google heavily uses data to optimize the potential of its employees. As Kathryn Dekas, Google's people analytics manager explained, "All people decisions at Google are based on data and analytics."[5] The company continually tests ways to increase people's physical presence at work and their well-being in the office. It even has retention algorithms that predict which employees are more likely to leave the company. Google has turned HR into a science.

A Fertile Environment

From the outset, Google has given itself a strong, well-defined culture, which is not the case in many companies born in the digital era. Some founders have even been described as *anti-leaders* for having created a workplace that is judged to be too tough.

Elon Musk, Travis Kalanick, and Jeff Bezos have been criticized for their callous ways of managing, which have been decried as being devoid of empathy for their employees. Jedidiah Yueh underlines, "One of the great ironies of the technology world today is how such broken people can create such perfect products."[6] The explanation comes from the fact that, for the leaders of these companies, conceiving and selling a great product is the only thing that matters.

Many have launched their own companies without having ever worked someplace else. They never rode up the corporate ranks to learn how to run a company—or to know what it's like to be an employee. Finally, they have not considered what a culture built on openness and integrity could bring, although it would be a good thing if they did. All the more so since, as Jedidiah Yueh says, with a bit of exaggeration: "Anti-leaders power the technology world. And the technology world rules the business world."[7]

An opaque company with strict hierarchical organization will inevitably confront difficulties. Transparency, entrepreneurship, equality, autonomy, collective resolution of problems, and open communications are valued more today than in the past. We are living in a more horizontal, collaborative world where culture should occupy an essential place because it gives life to sentiments and perceptions that don't come down from on high. Google's management understands that it cannot impose values like optimism, confidence, creativity, cohesion, or agility, but it can create a fertile environment that encourages these values to thrive.

We should not, however, mistake Google as being an idyllic company. Google is the target of attacks from across the globe. There is a gap between its internal and external images. The California company has struggled to bounce back from criticism on the issues of transparency, of its monopolistic position, and of tax evasion, all of which have harmed its public image. Personally, I have trouble with its unconstructive position on authors' rights.

But none of this affects the way Google's employees feel about their company. As we all know, Google is, in reality, much more than an Internet search engine. The company is working on driverless cars, carbon-emission reduction, robots, education, and artificial intelligence, not to mention the scientific research conducted into prolonging life expectancy. Google Venture, a growth accelerator, invests in at least one new enterprise every week. All this reinforces the pride employees have in their company. Google's staff remains the company's first and most fervent supporter.

It's interesting to see how Google, a firm from the austere and quantitative world of data, has been able to build something so qualitatively unique in such a short time. Google's culture is one of openness, autonomy, decision sharing, and success—to such a point that many members of Generation Y, with their limited and recent knowledge of the corporate world, actually believe that Google is a pioneer in corporate culture.

CHAPTER 11

PATTY MCCORD

ON EMPLOYEE EMPOWERMENT AND TALENT MANAGEMENT

As we've just seen, Google has a strong set of values. It decided to encapsulate them into a catchy motto: "Don't be evil."[1] This phrase, deeply incorporated into the company's culture since early 2000, has been part of its code of conduct that it communicates to its employees. In May 2018, the company adopted an adjusted version, which is now "Do the right thing."[2] By keeping this at the forefront of its people's minds, Google continues seeking to influence its workers' daily behavior.

Netflix also gives advice to its people. Here is a long list of counsels given by Patty McCord, former Chief Talent Officer:

- Be quick to admit mistakes.
- Say what you think even if it's controversial.
- Keep us nimble by minimizing complexity.

- Re-conceptualize issues to discover practical solutions to hard problems.
- Only say things about fellow employees you would say to their face.[3]

A few years ago, McCord described the culture of her California company in a 124-slide PowerPoint presentation. Sheryl Sandberg, number two at Facebook, gave praise by calling it "the most important document ever to come out of the Valley."[4] These slides have since been viewed more than 18 million times.

In this presentation, McCord explains that Netflix wants to grow fast, but without losing the values and effectiveness of a small structure. For her, "Most companies curtail freedom and become bureaucratic as they grow."[5] With growth comes complexity. To protect themselves, big organizations implement procedures that may optimize operations, but hinder creativity. For Netflix, the best way to grow is not by applying rules, but rather by hiring the most brilliant people. The company looks for people who work on their own, but are fully aligned to the company's objectives, which they know down to the slightest detail.

Netflix's deck on corporate culture insists on the values of freedom and responsibility. As Reed Hastings, Netflix's CEO and co-founder, says, the key lies in giving employees the power "to make their own wise decisions on behalf of the organization."[6] In an interview with Chris Anderson, TED's curator, Hastings explains that the company's success is due to the fact that so many decisions are taken at lower levels. "I pride myself on making as few decisions as possible in a quarter. There are some times I can go a whole quarter without making any decisions,"[7] he even went as far as saying.

Disruptive HR Practices

Many of Netflix's practices are unique. For instance, Netflix has no set policy for paid vacations. There are no policies for expenses, no bonuses, no annual evaluations, and no career plans. At first, this may seem astonishing but Netflix's management sees it as common sense, and perhaps one day other companies will as well. It's already the case for some French start-ups.

People work at home, in the evenings, and on weekends, replying to e-mails at all hours of the day and night. Considering this fact, McCord asked herself why Netflix should count annual vacation time if it doesn't count the hours people actually work. The company believes it should focus on what people do, not the number of days worked. That is why there is no policy for vacations. The number of days taken is left up to each employee to decide. This idea might be judged as utopian anywhere other than in Silicon Valley, where the culture of performance runs so deep that no one would consider abusing it.

Netflix is unusual in almost all aspects of its company life. Another surprising fact is that there exist no pre-set rules about expense accounts or travel. Some staff travel in business class, while others choose economy, but they all book their own tickets and choose the best fares, even though the company pays. Netflix doesn't use the services of a corporate travel agent. Its policy is contained in just five words: "Act in Netflix's best interests."[8]

The company gives no kind of incentive or bonuses because it believes that its people are all top achievers, and so money alone cannot make them want to work more or better. Employees have access to stock options, but not in addition to their salaries. If they want to purchase shares, they have to accept an accompanying salary reduction. It's up to employees to decide with their families on the best balance of compensation. Unusually, these stock options have no vesting period, so they can be cashed in immediately, which is another way Netflix is radically different from other companies. Its management is against the idea of imposing a years-long vesting period with the goal of building employee loyalty. The firm thinks taking its people hostage financially doesn't make sense.

At Netflix, there are no formal evaluations. The company considers them to be generally too ritualized and too infrequent to support meaningful change. Instead the company encourages multiple catch-ups throughout the year. For Netflix's chief talent officer, performance improvement plans (PIPs), like those often used in other companies, are fundamentally dishonest. "They never accomplish what their name implies,"[9] says Patty McCord.

Finally, there are no career plans at Netflix. It's up to each individual to manage his or her career evolution and to show himself or herself smart enough to seize the frequent opportunities that present themselves in such a fast-growing company. Netflix believes that for an extraordinary career you need luck and talent—two things that the company cannot provide.

A Contrasting Culture

We may be intrigued by such a compelling culture, one that gives such value to individual talent, but that does not mean it should be idealized. The way in which this culture is actually manifested on a daily basis is ambiguous.

On the one hand, the search for excellence at Netflix is reflected in its desire to attract the best, be it external talent for occasional collaborations or internal staff. It hires the most renowned filmmakers. In 2018, it released movies directed by the Coen brothers, Martin Scorsese, and Steven Soderbergh.

Alfonso Cuaron's *Roma*, produced by Netflix, won the Golden Lion at the Venice Film Festival. On the other hand, the substantial investments it makes in the production of original content, $8 billion a year, leads Netflix to employ thousands of not-yet-famous professionals from the world of cinema. For many of them, as promising as it might seem, the collaboration with Netflix often gives rise to tough financial negotiations.

The platform has attained such power that it can dictate its own conditions. Netflix doesn't disclose the number of downloads of its series. With no precise knowledge of the audience, artists have to accept a limited royalty deal, one that is most often disconnected from any actual viewer figures. Now Netflix could argue that it permits hundreds of directors and actors to work on films that, without its support, would probably never see the light of day. This is also true.

As for its employees, they come to realize that Netflix's culture, which initially appears so attractive, is in reality not so kind and relaxed. On the contrary, it is so performance-driven that it has become inflexible. For instance, managers are frequently required to apply the "keeper test."[10] They have to ask themselves, "If one of my people were to leave for a similar job in a peer company, would I fight hard to keep her or him at Netflix?"[11] If the answer is no, an employee's fate is sealed; that person will be fired. People whose talents no longer fit, however much they may have contributed, are asked to leave. The rule at Netflix is that "adequate performance gets a generous severance package."[12]

No one knows this better than McCord. After 14 years as the head of human resources, she was let go in 2012. Despite being considered by many observers as one of the greatest innovators in her field, her skills were no longer integral to Netflix. The rules and principles she helped to create led to her eviction; proof that preserving a culture can carry a high cost.

CHAPTER 12

THE DISRUPTION COMPANY

ON CORPORATE CULTURE COMPONENTS AND DISRUPTION

I would like to conclude Part III with a corporate culture I know well, that of my own organization, TBWA. This might appear somewhat presumptuous. Whatever its impact and its weight in the business world, my company is more modest than many others that are covered in this book. In a chapter dedicated to corporate culture, how can I not describe the one I know best, the one I live daily?

The *Harvard Business Review* identified what it has called "the six components of corporate culture,"[1] vision, values, practices, people, narrative, and place. I will attempt to describe TBWA's culture in line with these six themes.

Vision, Values, Practices

The first element is vision. At TBWA, we define ourselves as The Disruption® Company. Those not familiar with TBWA's history and with its role in shaping the word *disruption* might be a bit surprised. They should know, however, that using the word *disruption* in a business context originated with our agency. We were also the first to give the term a positive connotation.

Many might consider *disruption* to have become an overused, even somewhat generic concept. But as I stated previously, what makes a vision great is not so much its originality as its authenticity. TBWA has been cultivating this vision for almost 30 years. Every day we must try to live up to the high expectations we have set with regard to our company's positioning. To do so, we must think disruptively, create disruptively, and act disruptively in everything we do. We must try to avoid anything that leads to linear or incremental growth. We seek disruption.

Consider now values. Annual reports are full of the values companies espouse. From one company to another, we frequently come across the same words peppered throughout their documents such as *integrity, adaptability, frugality, responsibility, accountability, competency, sustainability, flexibility, utility,* and *transparency* without forgetting *innovative spirit* and *sense of leadership*. These values are not original, but what matters is how present they are in the heart of a company.

TBWA's culture also relies on a set of values. They are described in three words that are in themselves not necessarily distinctive: *creativity, curiosity,* and *diversity*.

Of our three values, *creativity* comes first. Every single day we are looking for ideas that are fresh, smart, and simple. Fresh because so few ideas manage to emerge from the immense noise of global communication. Most have become inaudible, invisible.

Smart because we should never underestimate our audience. No one ever complains about an ad being too smart. Simple because, as our Apple campaigns have always demonstrated, the simpler, the more impactful.

Ideas do not come out of nowhere. They come from an understanding of the cultures we live in and of the audiences with whom we are talking. This is why *curiosity* is our second value. We want and expect our people to have hungry minds. And we do a lot to help feed them. For instance, every day of the week, we produce a different three-minute video describing particular micro-trends and what's becoming important in emerging crowd cultures. This provides great food for thought. The goal is to help our people find ideas that, as our chief executive officer, Troy Ruhanen, says, "locate and involve brands in modern culture."

Our third value is *diversity*. "Embrace diversity, it will hug you back,"[2] believes John Hunt, our worldwide creative director. While gender diversity is important to us, at TBWA diversity goes far beyond the executive positions occupied by women. In our organization, six of our largest offices—Los Angeles, New York, Toronto, Shanghai, London, and Paris—are managed by women. While having a diverse staff at all levels of an organization is important, we also take *diversity* to mean openness to others. We see the value in cultural blending. Each of our local offices is endowed with its own strong local character, and this enriches our work. It's no coincidence that our Los Angeles office was chosen by Steve Jobs and our Johannesburg office by Nelson Mandela. We know that none of us individually is better than all of us together. Troy Ruhanen said some time ago, "I need Paris to come into New York. I need Turkey to come into China. I need L.A. to come into Australia. That's how we've got to work."

This leads us to our own business practices. The *Harvard Business Review* identified practices as one of the six components that form company cultures. The Disruption Days we conduct with our clients are the most concrete manifestations of our culture. Each of these events brings together around 30 people, half from the client side, and half from the agency. Over one or two days, they follow a precise sequence of activities based on a series of rigorous exercises. Our network has 270 agencies around the world and each one has held at least five Disruption Days per year, meaning we will have organized at least 10,000 of these events so far. We estimate that more than 100,000 of our clients' employees have participated in them, from China to Brazil, from South Africa to Finland. It would be difficult to imagine a practice going further in bringing a company's culture to life.

People, Story, Place

People means talent. Agencies are among those kinds of companies that are not protected by patents and cannot lay claim to the exclusivity of a given service or product. The value they create comes from the work they do every day, and that depends on the sum of the talents they are able to bring together. In our company we look to recruit people with a real entrepreneurial spirit, *doers* with a taste for all things artistic. These are people for whom music, exhibitions, and street art hold no secrets, and who are versed in crowd cultures. Our employees feel at home in an environment built entirely around creative processes and people. And, because we expect each member of our collective, no matter their level of seniority, to have a real influence on the agency, we ask just a single question in our regular evaluations, "What is your impact on our business?" Anything else seems superfluous.

Moving on, the fifth element is narrative. The *Harvard Business Review* says, "Any organization has a unique history, a unique story. And the ability to unearth that history and craft it into a narrative is a core element of culture creation."[3] TBWA has its own history, which has shaped the company into what it has become. To fully appreciate this, it's worth considering that of all the mergers that have taken place in the world, across all industries, the vast majority has actually destroyed value. The advertising industry is certainly no exception. It's a cemetery of mergers. Our network is an exception.

Why? Because of our culture. Our company was built by bringing together local agencies recognized for a high level of creativity in their own markets. The reason these partnerships have worked is that the agencies involved all claimed very similar cultures to begin with. Indeed, they all voluntarily adopted the Disruption methodology, even though it came from an agency, at the time BDDP, which was one of the last to join the TBWA network. From one country to another, our agencies have all remained very different, each with its own distinct local personality. But the common language that bonds them, the Disruption methodology, brings a real cohesion to the collective that they make up and forges the strong cultural backbone of our company.

The *Harvard Business Review* proposes a sixth and final element that it calls place, which could also be described as *interior architecture*. We want the way our agencies look to reflect who we are. Many of our offices have interesting designs, one of the best-known being our former office in Los Angeles, the so-called Binoculars Building," conceived by Frank Gehry. In all our agencies around the world, we favor open spaces with impromptu meeting places that facilitate chance encounters. Office design should encourage such serendipitous collisions.

I would like to expand on this notion of place, of space. The philosopher Emil Cioran once said, "One does not inhabit a country; one inhabits a language."[4] Language is indeed our common home. Bill Taylor, editor and founder of *Fast Company* magazine, wrote in *Mavericks at Work*, "Because they think about their business differently, maverick organizations almost always talk about their business differently. They devise a strategic vocabulary that distinguishes them from their rivals."[5]

At TBWA, we have adopted words that we are alone in employing. Our thought process is founded on a unique road-map of convention, disruption, and vision. Every day, we talk about things like Disruption Live, Backslash, No Format, Tiger Academy, Sea Legs, Take the Lead, Media Arts Lab, Cultural Edges, Disruption Lab, and other terms that we use in our own particular way. Our shared vocabulary is the most eloquent reflection of our culture.

This is what I wanted to say about the culture of the company I belong to. This culture is not inherently better than another; it's just different. And it's pervasive, something we at TBWA share. Our culture drives everything—and it has made us The Disruption Company.

The Disruption Methodology

On May 1, 1992, I published a full-page ad in the *Wall Street Journal*, *Le Figaro*, and the *Frankfurter Allgemeine Zeitung* with a single word—DISRUPTION—as the title, which appeared in heavy type across five columns. The term *disruption* was hence employed in a business context for the first time ever. Since then, the word has been misused for anything and everything—and it's even been denigrated.

When we created the Disruption® methodology in 1991, we gave the word a precise and positive meaning, contrary to those who later used it to describe reversals, upheavals, and even destruction. Our goal is to help companies grow, to conceive disruptive ideas and strategies, and to develop disruptive business models that will help them achieve what Troy Ruhanen calls "a larger share of the future."

For us, Disruption is an upstream concept, whereas for others, it is only a means of observation, a grid to read events that have already occurred downstream. Others notice that a disruption has taken place, but we try to imagine and create disruption from the outset, pushing it upstream.

The method often leads us to re-examine a brand's strategy, and sometimes even a company's. It helps us become what all agencies strive to be: "growth consultants." But there are two particularities. First, unlike the big consulting firms, we imagine futures for the brands we work with that go beyond extrapolations of the past and comparative analysis. We are consultants who use imagination. Second, we actually make stuff. We create things. This not a minor detail. Making things is at the heart of all true transformation. The way a strategy is brought to life often reveals its true power.

To return to the concept of corporate culture in general, I would like to stress again that any manager that allows his company's culture to become diluted is depriving himself of an incomparable asset. This is what Richard Branson meant when he said, "No matter how visionary, brilliant, and far-reaching a leader's strategy might be, it can all come undone if it is not fully supported by a strong and spirited corporate culture."[6]

Or as Lou Gerstner, IBM's former CEO, stated: "Culture isn't just one aspect of the game—it is the game."[7]

PART
FOUR

DISRUPTIVE BRAND BUILDING

John Smale was chief executive officer of Procter & Gamble from 1981 to 1990. I saw him in his Cincinnati office just a few days before he retired. I was curious to know what he felt had most changed in the discipline of marketing during his career. He said that, for him, it was the very concept of the brand; what changed was the idea of what a brand is and what it can become. To explain, he told me that just a few weeks previously, a recommendation had been made to him to launch a toothbrush under the Crest brand. He had accepted it without hesitation. What's interesting is what he said next. As a young brand manager, he had made the same recommendation decades before and it was vigorously rejected. Such an idea collided with the absolute dogma that reigned at the time: Product and brand were inseparable. One brand, one product. One product, one brand. It was unthinkable to risk diluting the image of the established product, in this case Crest toothpaste, by introducing a line extension. It was simply prohibited.

It was a coincidence that just before he left, Smale was led to take a decision opposite to that taken by his management a few months after he joined the company. Between the start of his career and his retirement, Procter & Gamble's very rigid concept of the brand had profoundly and definitely evolved.

This anecdote is more eloquent than it might at first appear. It highlights the distance traveled in our understanding of what constitutes the contours of a brand. When John Smale started at P&G, the brand was nothing more than a name. You had to give a product a name to identify it. Brand values were simply reflections of the product's attributes. Ivory was a pure brand, like the soap that bares its name.

But launching a new brand is expensive. So, for reasons of cost-efficiency, marketers around the world began to group products together and launch them under an existing brand name. These products were typically judged to have compatible attributes to the brand in question. This became known as an *umbrella* brand. When working with Danone, I took part in endless discussions to decide which of the dozens of yogurt and dessert products could be brought under the brand's banner. Those not corresponding to the healthy profile of the brand, or those seen as being too gourmet, were attributed to another brand.

This was back in the 1970s. It was only then that thinking began in terms of brand portfolios and, as a consequence, of brand territories, essences, and equities. The brand was no longer the same thing as the product. Little by little it gave itself its own values, over and above those of the products it had under its wing. Coca-Cola became much more than a soft drink, Levi's much more than a pair of jeans, Nike much more than running shoes.

The ultimate example of this is demonstrated by Virgin. This brand stands by itself alongside the products and services it offers. Richard Branson looked to enter markets that were sleepy, protected, and paralyzed. He once said, "I love tackling lazy industries.[1]" And so he invested in a multitude of activities that had no other common thread than that they were all fossilized. From music stores to mobile telecoms, from radio to a railway company, from the airline industry to bridal salons, the only common link between Virgin businesses is Richard Branson. He is the brand.

Over and above the products they include, brands have become assets in their own right.

A 2010 study by Millward Brown[2] showed that for S&P 500 companies, intangible assets exceeded the value of their tangible assets. Otherwise put, their trademarks, management systems, and brands are now worth more than their factories and inventories. And Millward Brown also found that among all of those intangible assets, the brand often came at the top of the list. It confirms that "the brand accounts for more than 30 percent of the stockmarket value of these companies."[3]

The job of marketing is therefore not only to drive sales, but also to increase the value of the brand. Sales overnight and brand over time. To achieve this, marketers must give more substance to their brands. They need to do everything possible to unleash their potential. They need to make their brands really matter.

In this part, the first three chapters are dedicated to disruptive marketers who know how to do this. Marc Pritchard, Chief Brand Officer of Procter & Gamble, an old-economy company, is probably the most influential marketing person in the world today. Brian Chesky, founder and CEO of Airbnb, understood early on the importance of the brand. He was ahead of the many entrepreneurs of other big Silicon Valley companies. Lee Clow, one of the most renowned creative minds of the advertising industry, has always known how to make brands shine. For more than 30 years, he has been responsible for Apple's advertising.

The last two chapters focus on two women entrepreneurs who are not really marketers in the conventional sense of the term, but who certainly know how to give weight to their brand: Oprah Winfrey and Arianna Huffington. Both have profoundly disrupted their business environment and created highly valuable brands.

CHAPTER 13

MARC PRITCHARD

ON TRANSPARENCY, ACCOUNTABILITY, AND CREATIVITY

At the end of 2017, Marc Pritchard received yet another award, certainly among his most prestigious so far. *Marketing Week* consecrated him as 2017 Marketer of the Year.[1] It seems natural to me to acknowledge the chief brand officer at Procter & Gamble, which is not just the world's biggest advertiser, but is also known as "the business school" for brand managers. The Cincinnati firm has maintained the greatest influence on the world of marketing and advertising since it began 180 years ago. The Harvard Business School had still qualified P&G as the absolute reference in marketing up until the end of the last decade.

This unequivocal statement has been challenged because things have since changed. For 10 years, P&G has traversed a difficult period. It appeared for a while as if it had underestimated the exponential growth of e-commerce, as well as the explosion of mobile phone use. Its sales suffered and it lost market share. It had difficulty growing markets in which its brands are category leaders. There are 16 of these markets where P&G is number one, and in which it has brands with revenues exceeding $1 billion.[2]

Critics have targeted P&G's culture, which had permeated every corner of the company. In July 2017, the *Financial Times*[3] stated clearly that the company's culture was at the root of its problems. In their view, P&G needed to become, as we discussed in Chapter 4, more agile. I, however, do not believe culture should be seen as the main source of the company's problems. For me, the problems P&G faces are more structural than cultural. Far from being a handicap, Procter & Gamble's culture strikes me as being an essential asset. It can act as the lever to help it make the necessary changes.

I have worked for nearly 30 years in agencies where Procter & Gamble was a client and, through these relationships, I have been able to closely observe certain elements of its culture. First, I noted the degree to which rigor occupies a predominant place in P&G's approach to most things. I have never come across a company that separates so meticulously fact from opinion. I can also testify to the company's integrity. Procter & Gamble does not meddle with ethics. And finally, one can only applaud how well staff members cultivate an internal sense of belonging, which is based on the confidence they have in each other's capacities. All of these elements play a role in creating a strong feeling of team spirit. To succeed in making the structural reforms needed while staying true to its beliefs, the enterprise must have a solid base—which is best provided by none other than its culture.

Day after day, Pritchard participates in the transformation of his company, but he has also contributed to that of the entire industry. In my opinion, he has done this to a greater extent than any other executive. His speeches are picked up and commented on the world over. Two of them in particular have created a major impact. One is a wake-up call, the other a rallying cry. The first was delivered in Florida in January 2017 at the annual congress of the Interactive Advertising Board (IAB). He denounced the many shortfalls of online advertising and made a series of propositions intended to shake up the market. The other speech was delivered in 2010 at the annual conference of the Association of National Advertisers (ANA). There, he challenged businesses and their brands to raise their ambitions, to give themselves a higher purpose. These two speeches, and his numerous other interventions over the past 10 years, have made Marc Pritchard one of the most listened-to personalities in the world of marketing. According to *Adweek*, he has become the "standard-bearer"[4] of his profession, a title they bestowed in September 2017.

Leading Change in the Marketing World

In the speech he delivered to the IAB Congress, Pritchard exhorted the marketing industry to disrupt itself. He pleaded for transparency in the digital world, vaunted the merits of mass one-to-one-marketing, and encouraged the reunification of creative and media. He considers these three elements to be essential for achieving more effective and efficient brand building.

Pritchard decried the aberrations of the digital advertising world. As years have gone by, his company measured how most digital advertising is purely wasted. According to him, "As little as 25% of the money spent in digital media actually made it to consumers."[5]

He advises agencies to let go of "the archaic *Mad Men* model."[6] In Pritchard's view, the system of buying and selling media is obsolete and not in sync with the tech revolution— "antiquated,"[7] as he describes it. He has lost patience not only with advertising and media agencies, but also with the Internet giants. His attack on them is unprecedented. He condemns the almost absence of standard digital metrics and is astonished by the lack of accuracy of the measurement tools that do exist. He also takes a stand against fraud and lack of transparency, both of which are especially prevalent in digital ad media. Finally, Pritchard denounces the unique threats to brand safety that exist online. Brand messages can unintentionally turn up on sites that contain violent, heinous, or sectarian content.

Pritchard has initiated a collective movement to clean up what he calls the "murky media supply chain."[8] He incited all those in the marketing sector to rally around five objectives:

1. The adoption of homogeneous viewability standards
2. The verification of audience measurement by an accredited third party
3. Transparency in agency contracts
4. The eradication of fraudulent practices
5. An absolute vigilance in matters of brand safety

"P&G is taking action because it's good for consumers, good for our business, and responsible for the industry,"[9] he concludes. His demands have met with real resistance, in part because they challenge the business models of Internet giants. Despite this, Pritchard obliged the largest Internet companies such as Google and Facebook to better respect marketers' needs and forced them to open their "walled gardens."[10] As he underlined, the fact that "P&G is the world's largest advertiser does carry some responsibility, but it also carries some opportunity."[11] The weight of Procter & Gamble did count.

Pritchard's second big subject is mass one-to-one marketing. The exponentially growing volume of data, and analysis technologies to exploit it, will allow "mass reach, with one-to-one precision."[12] Investments in data management platforms permit sharper targeting, avoiding what Pritchard calls the "spray and pay"[13] approach to media. We have fully entered into the era of one-to-one marketing. A promised capability of digital, but not yet delivered, can finally be realized.

Highly precise marketing consists of analyzing every step consumers take along their path to conversion, and influencing them when they are at the moment closest to purchase. P&G works with Amazon's consumer ID database to ensure that its brands reach consumers at just the right moment. The goal is to compress the time between the moment consumers first interact with a brand and the moment they are ready to take action. More than 10 years ago, Marc Pritchard presciently professed that "every consumer touchpoint should connect to purchase."[14]

Pritchard's third subject of concern is the entrenched distance between media and creative. He judges this to be counterproductive. In the digital era it makes no sense to disassociate the medium from the message. Despite being part of a company that once encouraged the unbundling of media and creative, Pritchard now believes that the two should be reunited. I remember him telling me, "In the nineties, we made the wrong trade-off."

Regardless of the enormity of the task, reuniting media and creative is as vital for our industry as the digital transformation of its agencies. More and more of our clients demand it. Everything has to be brought together—media with creative, data with strategic planning.

I'm now coming to a concept that for decades was rarely associated with the Cincinnati company: creativity. P&G was known in the past for its inflexible marketing approach. It favored ads that were repetitive and stereotyped—but in the 2000s, it finally came to realize the importance of creativity. Around that time, P&G hit a turning point and changed its creative philosophy. As resolute as it was unexpected, the change eventually led to P&G being frequently awarded with Lions at Cannes. The company knew that, in the Internet era, any message that doesn't contain an element of entertainment is zapped or just ignored. Creativity, previously seen as optional by the company, became an obligation. What had always been considered superfluous had finally become essential.

This shift soon bore fruit. The Old Spice campaign "Smell Like a Man, Man" was universally well received. The corporate film "Proud Sponsors of Moms," a tribute to athletes' mothers, the unsung heroes of the Olympics, was a smash hit during the Vancouver Winter Olympics. These two campaigns helped Procter & Gamble be named Advertiser of the Year at Cannes in 2008. I was asked to make a speech at this festival. I called it, perhaps not surprisingly, "The Beauty of Big," and the theme was how big companies were matching, if not beating, small ones when it came to creativity. Since then P&G has not lost its touch, as is attested by the Tide Super Bowl campaign which in June 2018 was awarded the Grand Prix in the film category, again at Cannes.

Most consumers only have a few occasions to see online advertising messages, although a tiny fringe of the population is continually exposed. Pritchard sums up this observation with these words: "We had been reaching too few people too many times with too many ads."[15] In an environment where frequency is too low, only impact can compensate. Otherwise put, it takes creativity for ads to be effective. You only have to see the Old Spice or Tide films once to remember them. And they are so original that web surfers have given them a lot of mileage. In my first book[16], I explained that only the strength of the idea will compensate for the inevitable diminishing of frequency. Thirty years later, here we are.

Pritchard called P&G's fight to eliminate waste in the digital media supply chain a thorny and painstaking task he could have done without. But he is persuaded that the five measures he encouraged the business to take have helped clean up the area he describes as "crappy advertising." [17] Because of this, he feels we may now be ready for a true explosion of creativity. This echoes his plea made at the October 2016 ANA's annual Masters of Marketing Conference in Orlando, where he encouraged marketers to "create the very best advertising the world has seen."[18]

Making Brands Serve a Higher Purpose

The marketing industry needs its own sense of purpose to create positive change across society as a whole. This was Pritchard's message to marketers at the Advertising Week conference in New York in October 2018. In a message that echoed the ANA speech he gave eight years earlier, he came back to the concept of purpose into the world of marketing. The idea itself was not new; Peter Drucker had evoked it 40 years ago. Other companies before P&G had also referred to it by then. But Pritchard is of those who has given new energy to the concept. He concurs with Richard Branson, who recently declared, "Brands that will thrive in the coming years—both financially and in terms of their impact on the globe—are the ones that have a purpose beyond profit."[19]

For almost 10 years now, P&G has given itself the purpose of "Touching lives, improving life."[20] The company is committed to spreading this purpose across the globe, now and for generations to come. The phrase might seem a bit generic, but the company genuinely thinks differently about its role in the world today. P&G wants to have a voice that counts on important matters such as diversity and inclusion, environmental impact and sustainability.

As well as the overarching purpose P&G has given itself at the corporate level, each of the company's brands, from Old Spice to Pampers, from Tide to Always, has its proper purpose. Always is a striking illustration of how powerful a purpose can be for a brand. "Empower girls and women."[21] I have chosen the Always example, even if it's well known, because the expression of its purpose is founded from the outset on one of the most universal insights a brand has ever exploited: the fear of failure.

A global study revealed that, all over the world, the stereo-types linked to gender affect girls most when they reach puberty because that is the moment when the differences between boys and girls are amplified and become more perceptible. Leader-ship, power, and strength, for instance, are associated with boys, while fragility, weakness, and emotionalism are associated with girls. These prejudices end up negatively altering the perception girls have of themselves, which affects their behavior. They lose their self-confidence.

The brand took on these stereotypes, using the expression "like a girl." This phrase is often used pejoratively to describe someone seen as being too feeble or emotional, but Always trans-formed it into a positive statement. The brand held a simulated casting session with young men and women and prepubescent girls and boys. The participants were asked to run or fight "like a girl." Young men, women, and little boys imitated girls running or fighting in a weak way, acting in stereotypical behavior that presents women as weak. But the pre-pubescent girls reacted completely differently. They ran and fought as hard as they could, with confidence, pride, and conviction. Cleary, their perception had not yet been formatted by prejudice and stereotypes.

The #LikeAGirl campaign has been seen more than 90 million times at the time of writing, and became the number-two viral video globally. In a study conducted after the campaign was launched, 76 percent of people said they perceived the expression "like a girl" to be positive after watching the videos, while only 19 percent had that impression before watching. Who would have believed that a brand of sanitary pad, usually a low-involvement category, would drive such huge levels of engagement? Herein lies the interesting thing about a sense of purpose: It is a concept that can apply to any product, however it touches life. The most everyday products—a dishwashing liquid, a detergent, or a sanitary napkin—can have a sense of purpose. There are no exceptions, even in the industrial world. Let's take the example of Air Liquide, a French world-wide leader in the production of industrial gasses. The company gave itself the purpose of "making the town breathe better."[22] Air pollution, accelerated through climate change, has become one of the principal factors of mortality in cities around the world. Air Liquide has invented processes that allow millions of people in cities to enjoy better air quality. The company does not just sell excellent industrial gasses, but it also concerns itself with vital environmental issues. Air Liquide wants towns to be able to breathe.

Coming back to P&G, I was invited to Cincinnati a few months after Pritchard's speech to attend a seminar on the theme of *purpose*. All the brand leaders gave presentations on the purposes they had assigned to their respective brands and it seems to me that the company doctrine on the subject has since become quite refined. Pritchard is more than ever certain that "if the purpose is disconnected from your business model, then it's not sustainable."[23] Among the whole panoply of causes P&G has embraced, it is up to each brand to evaluate the one that best fits its particular personality in the most meaningful way. What cause makes the most sense for it?

The delicate balance in the allocation of marketing resources has then to be determined. As a former P&G executive commented, "Purpose-inspired growth is a wonderful slogan, but it doesn't help allocate assets."[24] Looking for values of a higher order is so involving that it could lead the over-enthusiastic marketer to lean too heavily on brand purpose and lose sight of product performance. Always was able to avoid this trap. On the one hand, the brand pushes as hard as possible on its purpose to empower women and girls across the world. On the other hand, it continues to advertise the qualities of absorption and durability of its products. As such, the brand is both purpose driven and product led. Achieving this balance is a matter of dosage—how resources between the two levels are allocated—which reinforces the idea that purpose must emanate in some way from the product. The bond between purpose and benefit should be self-evident.

Years have passed since Pritchard's 2010 speech and his rallying cry has not escaped the fate of many widely circulated messages. Words, having been used indiscriminately, often inaccurately, can end up being robbed of their original meaning. Like *disruption*, *purpose* is one of these words. As of 2013, *Advertising Age* ran an article entitled "Is the Era of Purpose-Driven Ads (Finally) Over?"[25] The pervasive usage of the word has made it a staple of marketing jargon. It has become a buzzword.

And yet, I believe the concept has never been more relevant. Purpose reinforces the essence of the brand. It enriches a product's benefits by surrounding it with context. It associates the brand with a motivating social cause. From the moment a brand is given a clear sense of purpose, it has fuel for being inventive in what it does and in how it communicates about what it does. A great purpose gives a brand a disproportionate share of voice.

Confirming Pritchard's viewpoint, the Kantar "Purpose 2020" study[26] conducted in April 2018, shows that "brands with a high sense of purpose have experienced a brand valuation increase of 175% over the past twelve years, compared to the median growth rate of 86%." In broader terms, the value of brands with purpose grows twice as fast as the average. The findings speak for themselves.

CHAPTER 14

BRIAN CHESKY

ON BRAND BUILDING AND DISRUPTIVE DATA

Airbnb does not settle for just putting guests in contact with hosts; it dreams of a world where anyone can belong anywhere. A world without strangers, now that's a promising purpose. A little bit of utopia can't do any harm.

When Brian Chesky first met venture capitalists in the summer of 2008, none believed for an instant in his project. Chesky recalls, "People did not think strangers would stay with other strangers. They thought it was crazy." One of the investors even went as far as saying, "Brian, I hope that's not the only idea you're working on."[1] These doubts did not stop Airbnb from launching the first peer-to-peer accommodation platform and becoming the huge success we know today. To summarize Chesky, this was accomplished by "bringing the world back to the place where it feels like a village again."[2]

Since 2008, 150 million travelers have stayed in three million different hosts' homes in nearly 200 countries. The company is now present in 34,000 cities.

It took Chesky great resilience to achieve this. He needed to overcome the tempestuous opposition of numerous towns, involving legal battles against all sorts of prohibition. And it looks as if this will be a never-ending struggle. Following a series of incidents, he had to completely change his strategy in just a few days and, contrary to what he said previously, he declared himself partially responsible for what happens in hosts' homes. Finally, after a case of racial discrimination in North Carolina, he quickly established company policies, some of which went much further than federal law requires. The company always tries to tackle complaints head on, whatever sort they may be. The future of its business model depends on it.

I chose to talk about Chesky in this chapter for two reasons. First, he is the very archetype of the disruptive thinker. His home-sharing company has shaken the hospitality business from top to bottom. Second, in Silicon Valley, where the word *marketing* does not always get good press, he has managed, in a few years, to build an iconic brand, one that was reportedly valued at $31 billion as of March 2017.

Shaping an Iconic Brand

At the beginning, adopting a brand-building approach may not have been the obvious route for Chesky. As *Fast Company* explains, "There is a belief in much of Silicon Valley that you don't need to invest in brand marketing because your product itself is the brand."[3]

And yet, after initial success with early adopters and word of mouth, the time came to scale up the business. To accomplish this, Airbnb had to evolve from appealing almost exclusively to metropolitan hipsters—people who think it's cool to use the brand—to more lucrative audiences like young families or baby boomers. These groups still needed to be convinced. Neil Barrie, co-founder and managing partner at 21st Century Brands, comments, "You need a whole different set of tactics and tools to do that. Every brand faces that moment when they have to cross the chasm."[4]

This is a vital step for brands, like Airbnb, that are not protected by any patented technological IP. Having a strong brand helped the company to outperform competitors such as Expedia or Priceline, and to protect itself from the many start-ups trying hard to invade its market space.

For a few years now, Airbnb has been using advertising to illustrate the mission it has adopted: "Create a world where anyone can belong anywhere."[5] The brand's campaigns told travelers they could act as locals. In one of the commercials, the voiceover gives visitors this advice: "Don't *go to* Paris. Don't *tour* Paris. And please don't *do* Paris." After a montage of selfies and of the city's most famous landmarks, the ad concludes by encouraging viewers to "*Live* in Paris."[6] That Airbnb campaign was the first time the company was able to describe what it actually does in a simple and appealing way. As Nancy King, its director of brand strategy, pointed out, "That was the first example of product and marketing, two sides of the business, working together against a shared idea."[7]

To further substantiate its brand idea, and to continue capturing the attention of young generations, Airbnb is always pursuing novel initiatives. For example, in July 2015, when Cuba and the United States restored diplomatic relations after 54 years, the company launched its "No Borders"[8] campaign. It announced that 1,000 Cuban homes were available for booking and it published a full-page ad in leading newspapers like

The New York Times comparing this significant moment to another historical one, when mankind first set foot on the moon. The ad, which features America's and Cuba's respective flags side by side, read: "One giant leap for man's kindness."[9] President Barack Obama's endorsement helped turn Airbnb's initiative into a great business opportunity. The number of Cuban hosts grew from 1,000 to 4,000 within a year.

More recently, Airbnb initiated another very promising marketing idea. It rolled out new in-app features, which help travelers get a real taste of what day-to-day life is like for people who actually inhabit the cities they will be visiting. Airbnb guidebooks are fueled and filled by locals, not tourists. Unlike TripAdvisor, where clients rate the hotels, in Airbnb's guides, locals help users discover what there is to know about their neighborhoods. This creates a second-to-none experience and gives Airbnb a broader role, going well beyond just connecting hosts and guests.

Airbnb has thus joined the ranks of iconic brands such as Coca-Cola, Nike, Starbucks, and Disney, to mention just a few, which are admired both as businesses and social phenomena. They have become cults, because each, in its own way and at a moment in time, has impacted popular culture. They have known how to be in sync with their times. Today, it's up to other brands to have a chance of becoming legends. Apple, which ruled the start of the century, comes to mind first, but Facebook, Google, and Airbnb are close behind.

Airbnb's business model is so disruptive and appreciated by its users that you might say the brand was already iconic before it started advertising. That's possible, but I believe that the advertising the brand created helped accelerate its path toward iconic status. For a company that doesn't own its main tangible asset—rooms for rent—the ad campaigns have added value to what does constitute its most valuable intangible asset: its brand.

The Single Disruptive Data

Every step a consumer takes on the path to conversion is scrutinized: completing a lead-generation form, downloading an app, clicking on a cookie, using a voucher code, viewing a video, liking a Facebook page, visiting an e-commerce platform. Brands collate every kind of action imaginable: logins, friends' requests, clicks, page views, search entries, and so on. To manage all this information, marketing now relies heavily on data science.

Airbnb is no exception. It uses big data to enhance user experience. Ricardo Bion, the company's data science manager notes, "Airbnb is a data-informed company. We think data is the voice of our customers."[10] For instance, Airbnb provides price tips to hosts so, like hotels, they can charge higher prices when demand is strong and lower rates when it is not. Airbnb's user interface also allows hosts to establish price ranges they are willing to accept. Another algorithm predicts the likelihood of a host accepting a visitor's booking inquiry. The model learns from past decisions to predict future ones. There is no limit to how Airbnb can put to use the tons of data it gathers every day, from both hosts and guests.

This is what all Internet giants do. Uber constantly geolocates its clients and is aware of all their daily movements. Amazon can predict its customers' future purchases and prepare their packages, even before they've placed their orders. Netflix knows, ahead of its viewers, which films they are going to enjoy.

Apart from all the positive benefits of big data, there is also the risk of companies becoming submerged by the data flood. The *Harvard Business Review* issued this warning in one of its articles: "Don't let Big Data bury your brand."[11] This is a particular danger for companies using a disproportionate amount of data to drive purchases. Beyond pushing sales, data can serve as a great lever for brand building when it's used wisely. The great opportunity does not just come from exploiting, aggregating, and visualizing tens or even hundreds of bits of data. The real challenge—and route to success—is to isolate that single piece of data that will influence everything and help identify the insight that will guide the building of the brand. Dove's "Campaign for Real Beauty," which seeks to boost women's self-esteem, is a perfect illustration. Dove's marketing is based on discovering the insight that only 4 percent of women said they found themselves beautiful.

Having such data gives you a game-changing springboard. It's why I call it *disruptive data*, data that is decisive, pivotal, and critical. Procter & Gamble's Always is another example of this. Seventy-five percent of young women, upon reaching the age of puberty, say that the social networks where many users brag about their successes only serve to feed their own sense of failure.

In Belgium, CBC Bank discovered that people looking to buy a new house want to know everything about their future home and also all about the new environment in which they are going to live. For 82 percent of them, the neighborhood is as important as the house itself. This led CBC Bank to create the "Sleep on it" platform, where future buyers can learn more about their future neighborhoods before buying their home. They can get information about schools, shops, public transportation, and the average age and demographic profile of their future neighbors. They can also test the neighborhood by choosing to stay in a local Airbnb rental property, with one free night offered by CBC Bank.

Another example of insightful data use comes from Nike. The brand has commissioned a survey[12] that reveals that, in the United States, today's youth are the first ever generation that, due to their unhealthy lifestyle, are expected to die five years younger than their parents. This is the disruptive data that inspired the "Designed to Move"[13] campaign. The commercial features 20 children who describe what they would do if they had five extra years to live. The answers ranged from funny to profound. They would build a time machine, make medicine for the sick, go to the moon, get more hamsters, try to win five sports championships, go looking for aliens, fix the bad things they had done, and sing in front of a million people. "Designed to Move" is much more than just a campaign; it has actually generated a movement. As long as we do our part to stay in good health, we can put life expectancy back on the increase.

This notion of "disruptive data" echoes what Jedidiah Yueh calls the "magic metric" in his book *Disrupt or Die*. He explains how Facebook, in spite of gathering billions of elements of data, had become "data-rich and insight-poor."[14] This changed from the moment the social network distilled all the data down to a single actionable metric: seven friends in 10 days. A Facebook user who is joined by seven friends in 10 days is shown almost always to become a user for life. Since Facebook discovered this data, everything it does focuses on helping users reach that milestone.

Facebook identified its disruptive data point when it only had 40 million users, a number dwarfed by MySpace's 115 million. Discovering the "seven friends in 10 days" number was, according to Yueh, a key accelerator in the social network's success. He informs us that others have also found their magic metric. Twitter, for instance, wants users to follow 30 people. Zynga implements a "day one" retention policy to ensure users come back the day after signing up. Slack found out that if a team sends 2,000 messages, it is likely going to become a long-term user, a threshold that has been reached by 93 percent of Slack's customers. Companies that have identified their own metric can then work on ways to achieve their particular thresholds. "Divining a Magic Metric can enable terrifying growth,"[15] concludes Yueh.

In Silicon Valley we have seen that companies like Google and Netflix are committed to building strong corporate cultures, unlike many other organizations there that remain skeptical of promoting culture internally and externally. Similarly, by building a strong iconic brand, Airbnb is showing the way to non-believers of the new economy.

Among companies of the digital era, Airbnb is a pioneer in brand building. It can also serve as an example for companies in any other sector. Few brands master their own storytelling as well as Airbnb, and that is undoubtedly one of the reasons for its incredible performance. According to Kantar, since 2014, Airbnb has multiplied the value of its brand equity by 2.7 times.[16]

CHAPTER 15

LEE CLOW

ON THE POWER OF GREAT ADVERTISING

Lee Clow is the quintessential advertising man. For nearly five decades he has been the creative head of the leading agency in California. And he has been at the origin point of a great many iconic campaigns for brands such as Pedigree, Adidas, Nissan, Visa, and Apple. The spot used for the 1984 launch of the Macintosh has been celebrated by the advertising industry as the most admired commercial of the last century. And the series of 66 "Mac versus PC" commercials was named as the best campaign of the first decade of this century.[1]

It was Clow who also conceived the famous film signed "Think Different," which was dedicated to the "crazy ones who are crazy enough to think they can change the world."[2] The film is full of trailblazers including Einstein, Gandhi, Picasso, Martin Luther King Jr., and others. As Steve Jobs explained on his return to the company, this commercial made it clear to investors, observers, and employees that there was absolutely no way his company was going out of business.

Lee Clow was Steve Jobs's advertising partner since the very first days of Apple. In referring to him, Jobs once said, "He's the best guy in advertising."[3] For most people in our industry, Lee is a living legend and a guiding force.

Clow loves ideas in all shapes and forms, ideas that change the way advertising works, ideas that redefine creativity. He believes ideas accelerate change; they rule the world.

Big Brand Ideas

When it comes to our business, Clow likes to say, "Big ideas win. Good ads don't." More than being a criticism of "good ads," his comment should be seen as an encouragement to always associate brands with powerful ideas. This is what he calls "big brand ideas."

He knows better than anyone how to encapsulate in just one or two words the essence of a brand, be it Apple, Nissan, Adidas, or Pedigree. He was at the genesis of lots of big brand ideas, including Apple's "Think Different," Nissan's "Shift," Adidas's "Impossible Is Nothing," and Pedigree's "Dogs Rule." These are ideas of a higher order, the kind that Marc Pritchard at P&G has always looked to promote. Pritchard is a strong believer that "big ideas are the currency of our industry. They lift the entire brand."[4] As for me, I have always thought that such ideas establish a before and an after in a brand's life.

Our industry is at its best when clients take ownership of the advertising slogans we create for them. On his return to Apple, Steve Jobs stressed the importance of "Think Different" to an audience of retailers. Erich Stamminger of Adidas declared in front of a crowd of enthusiastic staff members that "Impossible Is Nothing." As for Nissan's Carlos Ghosn, he mentioned "Shift" at several automobile shows, held in cities from Tokyo to Detroit. In referring to these ideas, business leaders use advertising words to show the world how they see their companies.

Some people think that this way of viewing our business is out of date, that the importance given to the brand idea is a vestige left over from the old school. The evolution of technology and data is such that many believe that advertising will now only focus on driving transactions and promoting sales. It's true that automated, digital, transaction-driven advertising will be the fastest-growing marketing activity in the coming years. But it's worth underlining that the way this kind of advertising is conceived does not naturally lead to great, overarching ideas. Its mission is rather to deliver a multitude of specific messages to very narrow targets. Of course, this type of advertising is indispensable but, at the same time, it can result in fragmented brand experiences and an increasingly diluted overall brand image. Which is why I think that, today more than ever, expressing an overarching idea about what the brand stands for remains a priority.

One of the brand ideas I just mentioned dates from 1998; the others are from the middle of the 2000s. I thought at the time that such big brand ideas would start to flourish and I was on the lookout for them everywhere. I observed ideas from agencies all over the world—our own and our competitors'—but ideas of this style and magnitude rarely took hold, because most creative people today are looking for ideas of a different nature, which they can exploit in real time and circulate instantly on the web. These may be really creative—"good ads," as Clow would say— but they nevertheless remain somewhat narrow ideas. They lack the stature of brand ideas. The growing importance of digital has dragged our profession in another direction.

When I talked about the merits of brand ideas, I sensed that creatives were skeptical. They thought I was having trouble letting go of something that had worked well in the past. But then, little by little, these brand ideas started to reappear. Among those from Clow's agency, I can cite Gatorade's "Win from Within," Reuters' "The Answer Company," Accenture's "New Applied Now," and Airbnb's "Belong Anywhere." Nike is another example. For more than 10 years, Nike's agency, Wieden & Kennedy, had stopped closing its commercials with one of the most famous brand ideas ever created: "Just Do It." At the 2017 Cannes Lions, I was pleasantly surprised to see that tagline reappear on Nike's ads. Recently, a new Nike commercial featured Colin Kaepernick, the American football player who kneeled during the national anthem in protest against racism. In doing so, the brand drew strong criticism. The end of the film finishes with this voiceover, "Don't ask if your dreams are crazy. Ask if they are crazy enough. It's only crazy until you do it. Just do it."[5] This proves that if big brand ideas are kept fresh, they can span generations.

A big brand idea is, at the same time, a source of inspiration, and a filter. It gives direction to all the creative initiatives and outputs—videos, films, events, brand content, posts and tweets, conversations on social networks—that substantiate the idea, day after day. A brand idea also enables you to exclude messages that do not reflect what the brand really stands for, no matter how creative or interesting they may be. Digital disperses messages and attention. Brand ideas do the opposite. They provide focus. They aggregate.

Brand ideas bring more density and substance. They give a sharper image. They create a new moment in a brand's history. They simplify solutions to complex problems. They often accelerate change, but always add value. The value of the Nike brand, which is listed as its prime asset on its balance sheet, represented almost 30 percent of the company's total market capitalization[6] in December 2018. And whereas it's not possible to measure precisely the contribution of the "Just Do It" idea, it unquestionably counts for a lot.

Creativity, the Advertiser's Best Bet

All this being said, and irrespective of finding big ideas or not, we are living in a media environment that is in constant upheaval. Media and business analysts are alarmed by what they refer to as "the progressive disappearance of audiences." In fact, rather than speaking of disappearance, it would be more accurate to describe dispersion and fragmentation. Audiences have not disappeared but, because of the vast number of content choices, they have become scattered and difficult to reach.

To compound this, tens of billions are being invested by platforms like Amazon or Netflix to produce quality programs. By allowing their subscribers to avoid seeing advertising, they also contribute to audience erosion. The advertising business is experiencing a significant reduction in the consumption of traditional media, and it must find new ways of reaching those referred to as the "unreachables."

Guillaume Pannaud, the head of our French agency, sums up the challenge our industry is facing: "Our job consisted in creating messages to reach an audience. Now we have to create audiences." To do so, marketers need to aggregate the thousands of Internet users who are interested in the content their brands produce and make them want to share it. But viewers will only circulate content that they find original, new, surprising, uplifting—in a word, *creative*. In this age of ad clutter, ad blocking, and ad avoidance, there is no place for mediocre work.

On a positive note, brands today have a great many levers to activate new ways of interesting their audiences. Creativity is taking on new forms. I've looked at the options that brands can use. Here's a list. Brands can exploit the compelling data they have isolated, or build on an insight they have uncovered. They can sink into a crowd culture where people share things centered on common interests. They can be inspired by the news or by conversations being conducted on social networks. They can take advantage of an event they have created, or one organized by someone else. They can propose brand tutorials, or use YouTubers' videos. They can produce online mini-documentaries showing the initiatives they're taking. All of these levers are new ways for brands to reach those "unreachables" and, in doing so, to touch the very core of their digital intimacy.

Nevertheless, an advertising message, in whatever form or channel, has always been—and always will remain—the fruit of the conjugation of two elements: an idea and the way in which this idea is expressed. The idea must be creative and so, too, must be the storytelling that brings it to life.

The ultimate value of an idea depends on the way in which it is executed. Imagining messages that are fresh and original requires a certain know-how, not to mention talent. Pritchard often speaks of the craft of advertising. "Express the brand as a masterpiece painted on a creative canvas,"[7] he says. We are always looking for the right phrase, for finely chiseled formulas. Whether it is in conceiving films, creating websites, or producing short programs, we must preserve this respect of the written word, this concern for things well done. Some would like to make our business an industry, but it must remain a craft.

This finally leads to a topic that has been crucial for me for decades: the relationship between creativity and effectiveness. There is proof of the direct link between them. Solid, statistical evidence[8] has been supplied by both the Gunn Report, a relent-less advocate for creativity, and the British Institute of Practi-tioners in Advertising, a well-respected organization with one of the richest databanks on effectiveness. The findings are unequiv-ocal: Creatively awarded campaigns provide a higher return and, paradoxically, with less risk.

McKinsey has also devoted two studies to the subject. The first states, "The more creative a campaign, the higher the likelihood that the featured product will sell."[9] The second study,[10] published in 2017, led McKinsey to observe that creativity matters for the bottom line. It would appear that the Boston Consulting Group and Bain share the same opinion. They agree with the McKinsey conclusion that "other things being equal, creativity is an advertiser's best bet."[11]

I imagine the Lee Clow of the 1960s, an avid surfer and raw creative talent. He would likely never have imagined that McKinsey would one day make such a statement, or that the best-established consulting companies would confirm what he's been trying to prove all his life: that creativity can be a real game-changer.

Clow pays attention to every word, every pixel, every pack, every logo, every little piece of point-of-sale material. For him everything counts because, as he says, "Everything a brand does is advertising."[12]

CHAPTER 16

OPRAH WINFREY

ON BUILDING A ONE-PERSON BRAND

The purpose of this book is to celebrate people whose influence has gone beyond the bounds of their own company. As such, it would have been difficult not to mention Oprah Winfrey and Arianna Huffington. They have had unparalleled success in the business of influence, and their brands resonate with people at a level rarely achieved before they came onto the scene.

I would guess that Winfrey and Huffington are no great fans of advertising. Despite this, following Lee Clow's thinking, a lot of what they do could be considered as *advertising*, or at least promotional. Each, in her own way, has patiently built a brand of very great value, in both symbolic and financial terms. Like Steve Jobs and Richard Branson, Winfrey and Huffington are the indisputable faces of their companies—but each one's name has become the brand. They embody what is now known as personal branding—and Winfrey, like Huffington, is a paragon of her time.

The Ultimate Celebrity Brand

Winfrey understood very early on that she was a brand—and she had strong intuition about how to progressively shape it. In doing so, she has become an iconic brand.

Some years ago, Airbnb and TBWA\Chiat\Day worked together on a research paper about what makes a brand iconic.[1] Their work indicates that truly iconic brands embody all five of these attributes:

1. They are instantly recognizable.
2. They create deep emotional connections.
3. They have a universal value proposition.
4. They play a role in culture.
5. They stand for higher-order values.

The Oprah brand excels when it comes to these five attributes. Let's consider each of them.

First, Oprah Winfrey's charismatic broadcasting style is not just due to the way she acts and the way she talks, but also to her physical presence. Hundreds of thousands of fans all over the world find her relatable. And yet, her first boss at WJZ-TV insisted she change her appearance—and, in a way, betray the reality of who she was. The story is well known. At the time, Winfrey was 20 years old. She was considered to be a bit overweight and she was not white, a combination that made her vastly different from the trendy television personalities of the time.

But one day the head of Chicago's ABC affiliate station assigned her the morning show. He "let Oprah be Oprah."[2] She succeeded in transforming what many had considered a disadvantage into the very foundation of her image. She never tried to be anything else than herself—and that became her strongest asset. From the very outset, Winfrey understood that success relies on defining herself instead of letting others define her.

Second, Winfrey creates deep emotional connections with her audience. She was not the first person to host a talk show on television, but she gave new meaning to the format. She brought a personal, almost intimate approach to a well-established, glitzy type of program. She knew how to create close ties with millions of people. The expressions that are most frequent when people describe her are: genuine, candid, real. She exudes honesty. It is her hallmark, and it's hard to think of another celebrity having built such a close degree of confidence with the public. This comes from always putting herself on an equal footing with her viewers, by opening up about her own personal vulnerabilities, and by addressing issues that were previously considered private. And in this way, she has always related to her guests in such a sensitive, emotional way that the camera cannot escape it.

This has been described by Time magazine as "*rapport talk*," and "an approach of personal dialogue, confession and compassion."[3]

For Winfrey, it all starts with an intention. By intending to become something, you have a better chance of succeeding. This is because our intentions, in addition to our actions, influence our realities. It's the firmness of intent that opens up new possibilities and allows us to approach the life we aspire to. This is why Winfrey always asked her guests to describe their intentions in life, and why she clarified her own intentions in inviting them to her show. It has become a structural element of her interviews.

Winfrey knows hundreds of celebrities and she has an astute observation on their role with brands: "While you can grow your brand with celebrity endorsement to capture attention, being real and engaging with everyday people will capture hearts."[4]

Third, Winfrey has always had a clear and compelling value proposition, encapsulated in the line "Live your best life."

This phrase is, as Lee Clow would say, a big brand idea. It's an encouragement to take care of ourselves, an exhortation to live our lives to the fullest. It's about self-growth and finding meaning. Since the beginning of the 2000s, dozens of articles on how to "live your best life" have appeared in *O*, Winfrey's magazine. The expression has become ubiquitous. A Google search on the phrase generates 6.1 billion results, including articles, social media posts, and websites dedicated to the subject.

Deep down, Winfrey's purpose is none other than to help people find the path between what they are and what they seek to become. It's a struggle for every one of us. This purpose is the constant across her media empire. And along the way she gives us lots of both insightful and down-to-earth advice. One example is tied to the theme of vulnerability: "Turn your wounds into wisdom." Among my favorites are: "Real integrity is doing the right thing, knowing that nobody's going to know whether you did it or not" and "You don't become what you want, you become what you believe." A final example is: "So go ahead. Fall down. The world looks different from the ground."[5]

Why do all these phrases stir us up? Not only because they light a spark when we hear them, but also because they clearly reflect decades of dedication, commitment, and tenacity. Personal branding takes time—25 seasons in the case of *The Oprah Winfrey Show*.

The fourth element of great brands is that they play a role in culture. This is obviously true for Winfrey. Mary McNamara, a leading TV critic from the *Los Angeles Times*, credits Winfrey with having made a major impact on culture as a whole. Among her contributions are her role as the catalyst for the genre of celebrity memoir and of journalists opening up to share their personal feelings and experiences with the general public. "You see it everywhere, from the explosion of memoirs to social media to journalists sharing their own opinions and own stories. That all started with Oprah,"[6] says McNamara.

Her work on her TV show, magazine, blog, and TV channel has immersed Oprah Winfrey in popular culture. At the same time she reflects it and shapes it. She has encouraged her audiences to exercise, to follow diets, to read, to become self-aware, to participate in community volunteering, and even to meditate. She has discussed women's empowerment, racial discrimination, gun control, the path to citizenship for immigrants, social justice, and freedom of the press. She does all she can to make her fellow citizens take interest in subjects that are too often hijacked by the elite or niche groups that hold special interests.

Last but not least, Winfrey was the first to air subjects that had previously been considered taboo. She has turned issues like protection of abused women and LGBT rights into everyday topics of discussion. Her speech at the 2019 Golden Globe Awards, where she vigorously denounced sexual assault, harassment, and gender inequality, has been a milestone for viewers all over the world. It ended with the statement of a firm belief that "a new day is on the horizon."[7]

Turning to the fifth element of iconic brands, Winfrey stands for higher-order values. Not only is she a great advocate for social causes, but she also acts on them. She has personally given back to society through her numerous philanthropic actions. She has always been discreet on the subject, but it's a fact that through the Oprah Winfrey Foundation, she has distributed more than $50 million of her own money. She has contributed to the education of thousands of underprivileged women and children, all over the world. She has also founded the Oprah's Angel Network to raise funds from her audience to support nonprofit organizations. She has built schools in several different countries, offered scholarships, and set up youth centers and shelters for women.

Oprah Winfrey contributes to what philanthropic organizations call the *promise of equity*,[8] which consists of reaching the most vulnerable people. This includes the poorest families, child victims, those plagued by ethnic or religious segregation, and people with handicaps—to name just a few who have always been left behind.

To sum it up, I would say that Winfrey has implemented the five elements of what constitutes an iconic brand in a way that has rarely been done before. Her work has created an extremely solid foundation for what has become a media empire. And other brands—not only personal ones—can follow her example.

For the record, and especially for those non-American readers of this book, it's worth remembering that her show had 44 million viewers a week in the United States, making it the highest-rated talk show in television history; it was broadcast in 145 countries. *O, The Oprah Magazine* has an average monthly circulation of nearly 2.4 million, making it one of the leading women's titles in her country. Oprah's Book Club has promoted many previously unknown authors, catapulting books onto the bestseller lists. It has become a real force in the publishing industry and is estimated to be responsible for sales of more than 60 million books. And it's important to remember Winfrey's highly successful film-production company, Harpo.

All of these achievements have made Winfrey a powerful voice in America and one of the most important female voices in the world. They have contributed to Oprah the person becoming Oprah the brand.

The One-Person Businesses

Many celebrities have attained the status of a worldwide brand. One that immediately comes to mind is Kim Kardashian, who has never denied making it her intended objective. But for others, it happened over time. You find personal brands in many different domains. In sports, there are of course Michael Jordan and Tiger Woods. But maybe the sector that has the largest number of personal brands is music, which includes artists like Michael Jackson, Beyoncé, and will.i.am. As Jay-Z puts it in one of his raps, "I'm not a businessman. I'm a business, man."[9]

In the last decade, more and more previously unknown people have begun to think of themselves as brands. Today we are observing the rise of "one-million one-person businesses." In 2015, according to the U.S. Census Bureau, 35,584 nonemployer firms earned between $1 and $2.49 million in revenue.[10] This was rendered possible thanks to digital developments, low-cost outsourcing, 3-D printing, automation, free access to software, and pay-per-click advertising.

Most often, the difference between these success stories relies upon the capacity of the individuals involved to brand themselves. The expression "personal branding" is not new; it was used by Tom Peters[11] back in 1991. But today, the issue is not so much to know if you want to become a brand, but rather if you have willingly decided to master the way you're going to build it. How will you control the impression you leave in the minds of others? How will you shape what people are going to think when they hear your name? What do you imagine could be your best digital footprint?

As we've seen from Lee Clow, who cares about every minute detail of the brands he's in charge of, everything counts. Each tweet you make, every picture you share, every post you write. Your brand image is an accumulation of many little things. Winfrey understood it intuitively right from the beginning. She controls absolutely everything that touches her brand, and even approves every page of *O* magazine before it goes to print.

Forbes[12] listed the best practices for becoming a successful one-person brand:

- Use digital tools to verify your hunches.
- Own a narrow niche.
- Put community happiness first.
- Pay attention to reviews.
- Know when to quit your day job.
- Learn basic technologies.
- Connect.

I would add one other point: Once you've defined what your image should be, you have to live up to it—and never try to be someone you are not. Authenticity like Winfrey's is of paramount importance for any one-person brand. Self-packaging must be genuine and true.

Influencers are a category of their own when it comes to one-person brands. They seek to capture and hold the attention of the segment of American 13-to-24-year–olds, who spend an average of 11.3 hours per week watching online videos.[13] Once the influencers have constituted their audiences, brands solicit them to conduct influencer marketing. Companies such as Maybelline or L'Oréal, for example, partner with bloggers to create tutorials on makeup. According to *Variety*,[14] one of the most popular entertainment publications, a YouTube tutorial with a star influencer can be up to seventeen times more engaging than a traditional celebrity tutorial.

Individuals are blending less and less into the collective. American statistics predict that in the near future, 40 to 50 percent of the U.S. workforce will be made up of independent workers.[15] These people are happier working alone, at their own pace, for multiple organizations. Many believe this work arrangement provides a richer experience than working for a single company. The best of these freelancers will become like brands. They will be in high demand and will have more work they can handle. Companies will compete to have access to them.

This gives me the answer to the question: Will the importance of corporate culture decline as a growing part of the workforce comes from the outside? The answer is no. It may seem paradoxical, but I believe that culture will remain as important as ever. The best outside talents will be attracted by the most seductive cultures. It's a company's unique way of thinking and creating, its distinct way of working, that will enable it to secure contracts with highly demanded talent. Every company will look to become the company of reference for these freelancers. It will be the determining factor when demand exceeds supply.

Great corporate brands will attract great one-person brands.

As for Winfrey, it's been said that, in the early years, she resisted being seen as a brand. She was always distrustful about anything to do with marketing, a discipline she found lacking in authenticity. She feared that becoming a brand would distance her from her fans. She explained that she changed her mind when she came to understand that her way of being and behaving, the elements that made up the Oprah brand, helped people to change their lives. The lesson for her was that a trustworthy brand "enables others to trust in you and to connect with exactly what you stand for and who you are." And she simply concluded: "Be your own brand."[16]

CHAPTER 17

ARIANNA HUFFINGTON

ON DIGITAL JOURNALISM AND WOMEN'S EMPOWERMENT

Three young Colombian entrepreneurs discovered a chemical process that can be used to turn plastic bags into bricks.[1] The bricks are solid, water resistant and cheap and are used in construction to build low-cost houses and schools. With this invention, the entrepreneurs have killed three birds with one stone. First, they permit poor women to earn a little money by collecting plastic bags that are often lying on the ground. Second, they contribute to the cleanup of the planet and oceans. And, third, they help to make home ownership possible for a great number of people. Of course the impact of these innovative bricks is still quite limited, but just imagine for a moment what could happen if it could be scaled up in all the little villages and cities of the world.

A lot of websites like *Good News Network* or *The Week in Good World News* are dedicated to promoting progress and advances in all kinds of different domains. But the site with arguably the greatest impact is the *Huffington Post* (renamed *HuffPost* in 2017). Its founder, Arianna Huffington, had become alarmed by the fact that people watching the news or reading the newspapers were faced with an appalling vision of the world we live in. Armed conflict, terrorism, financial crises, assorted crimes—all of this is our daily lot. Whereas it's obviously essential to keep people informed, for Huffington, the general impression created is too unbalanced. As she has said: "There are a lot of horrible things happening in the world but it is not 95% bad!"[2] This is why she decided to shine a light on people who are doing and inventing things to resolve the problems of our world. The *Huffington Post* focuses on actions that are constructive.

The impact of positive initiatives, such as the one from Colombia, may be limited, but Huffington considered it her duty to make them known. The media, she said, "should give them more oxygen." So she included on her site several sections like "What's Working," "Good News," and "The Best Feel-Good Headlines From Last Week." To quote the journalists at *Huffington Post*, "Any time you feel depressed, you can go there and feel optimistic about the world and human nature again."[3]

In this way, Huffington challenged what social media thrives on: the bad news that feeds the buzz. This is just one of the many innovations coming from the *Huffington Post*. As we will see, its entire model is disruptive.

The Consecration of Online Journalism

Back in 2005, the editorial staffs of the print media naively thought that confronting the Internet revolution could be accomplished simply by reproducing newspaper articles online.

Lots of more or less niche news blogs already existed, addressing narrow groups of readers. Then, along came Huffington. Her project was of quite a different dimension. Her online journal was simultaneously a media company and a collaborative platform. It was a news site based on interactions between journalists and Internet readers to a degree never before achieved. She knew she could harness the explosion of information. The amount of digital data produced online in 2006 alone was three million times the material of all the books ever written. "It only took six months for the *Huffington Post* to surpass the web traffic of the *Wall Street Journal*, the *New York Times* and the *Washington Post*."[4]

Huffington disrupted conventional journalism and gave respectability to digital news reporting. She did this in multiple ways. First, she understood very early on the importance of social networking and the role celebrities would play. When the *Huffington Post* was just beginning, she had no hesitation in flipping through her address book and asking people like George Clooney, Alec Baldwin, or Madonna to write for the site for free.

Then, after having called upon the stars, she opened up her site to the world, to the non-famous people who had something interesting to say. And she allowed them to publish their articles alongside those of the big-name authors. Thousands and thousands of people responded to such an opportunity. This unremunerated content generation, an unusual practice at the time, was the foundation of her economic model.

Huffington has been called the "Queen of Aggregation."[5] She knew better than anyone how to give new life to content that had already appeared elsewhere, often by expanding upon or reducing the coverage, and giving it a catchier headline. She even used a system of A/B testing between headlines to measure which would generate the most traffic. She told her detractors that this allowed her to give more visibility to the articles and to their authors, via the links she provided to the source.

Beyond external volunteer columnists, the site's editorial staff has been strengthened over time. It has counted up to 250 writers and reporters in 2017, some of whom have received prestigious journalistic awards and recognition. At the end of the day, Huffington has turned her site into an editorial meeting place for celebrities, journalists, and the general public. It is a perfect blend. More than just an aggregator, she was actually an incomparable gatherer.

She also understood better than anyone a major characteristic of online journalism. Not only does the news need to evolve in real time, but it also needs to be delivered in a particular way. Algorithms allow maximum interactivity with readers, leading to content being constantly fine-tuned and adjusted. As declared Kenneth Lerer, one of her associates, commenting on the fact that articles are always being reviewed and corrected, "digital is painting in oil."[6]

Huffington's critics have qualified her approach as being mercantile. It is true that she had a clear mind of what the general public wanted to read, and how to present it, and this often led to comparisons of *Huffington Post* with tabloids. I imagine she didn't pay too much attention to these remarks. Maybe she knew that Joseph Pulitzer and William Randolph Hearst were held in low esteem by established journalists. Yet, this didn't stop Adolph S. Ochs, who bought the *New York Times* in 1896, from paying tribute to them. He said: "Such papers as *The World* and *The Journal* exist because the public wants them. I hold that some of their features are open to criticism, but each of them has done infinitely more good than harm."[7] Over 100 years later, one can say without contest that Huffington did the same.

In 2012, the *Huffington Post* was awarded a Pulitzer Prize.

Women in Business

I wanted to evoke Oprah Winfrey and Arianna Huffington in this book, because they are both emblematic women entrepreneurs who have disrupted the business environments in which they operate. And each, in her own way, has battled for the equality of the sexes, for true emancipation of women, so that their voices may carry as powerfully as those of men.

I remember a campaign that ran back in the eighties. It was for a major French mail order company. The tagline my agency created stated that the future belongs to women. It sounds beautiful in French: "*Demain sera féminin*," meaning "Tomorrow belongs to women." It was written 30 years ago, and it is regrettable to note that *tomorrow* is still late in coming.

The glass ceiling is still there. Today in the United States, "men still hold 95 percent of the CEO positions and about 85 percent of all executive positions of Fortune 500 companies."[8] And in 10 years, the percentages have only shifted a point or two. This major gender imbalance is obviously highly distressing.

In 2014, the *Huffington Post* explained that "gender equality for women cannot happen without men."[9] And it exhorted its male readers to fully engage in pursuing equality between the sexes. No change can happen unless the men who are currently leading businesses truly accept that the promotion of equality is not just a moral obligation, but also a strategic necessity. Gender equality is not a nice-to-have, it is a business imperative.

Countless studies have demonstrated the point to which equality in the workplace increases productivity. Giving senior responsibility to women allows companies to better understand half of the world's population. This is pretty obvious. It also provides them the opportunity to acquire better insights into the people who make the majority of household purchasing decisions. Additionally, women own nearly half of the shares of publicly traded companies in the United States. You could ask yourself what the business world is waiting for to give them more access to senior positions.

A greater number of women are going to college. In the United States,[10] the percentage of female graduates in the labor force has risen from 11 percent in 1970 to more than 42 percent today. In most Western countries, women now surpass men in terms of postgraduate education. As we have all seen, when women join companies, they bring with them new, different ways of seeing things. They possess qualities that are indispensable to the world of business. We know that having diverse opinions and experiences around the table increases the chances of producing new thinking. Earlier in this book, I talked about the deficit of innovation that exists in a great number of companies. Increasing the number of women in decision-making positions should be one of the first responses to this deficit.

Things are, nevertheless, beginning to change, even in places where it's least expected, such as in Silicon Valley. In one *Huffington Post* article,[11] a contributor underlined that "women are the most disruptive force in tech." This is not just backed up by the cases of Sheryl Sandberg at Facebook or Marissa Mayer during her time at Yahoo! The author cites as examples the dozens of women on the rise in companies such as Twitter, Microsoft, Google, and Pinterest. Today, women are filling approximately half of the new tech jobs.

The same article pointed out that 200 women were founders or co-founders of the 125 most successful tech start-ups of the last decade, with stock-market capitalization above $50 million. Another striking statistic is that tech companies led by women have, on average, a 12 percent higher annual revenue than their equivalents led by men. These same companies required a third less capital employed to achieve these results. The time for pro-crastination is over. It has become urgent to permanently remove all barriers to equality.

Time goes on. In 2011, Huffington and other shareholders of the *Huffington Post* sold the company for about $315 million. This offers further proof, if needed, of the power of her business model. A few months later, she launched a new adventure: Thrive Global, a platform focused on health and wellness. She has developed work-shops and courses on work-life balance. This project continues the work Huffington started in two books she published, *Thrive* and *The Sleep Revolution: Transforming Your Life, One Night at a Time.*

She chose a subject that at first appears merely interesting, but it is actually crucial. It concerns the effects of lack of sleep, includ-ing stress. She denounces the illusion that to succeed, working people too often think that they should always be connected. She seeks to end the "macho culture of burnout and overwork."[12] She wrote an open letter to one man in particular—a familiar business figure who sleeps very little; works 120 hours a week; and spent his 47th birthday, all 24 hours of it, at work. The man is Elon Musk, and this is part of what she wrote to him:

> You're a science and data-driven person. You're obsessed with physics, engineering, with figuring out how things work. So apply that same passion for science not just to your products but to yourself. People are not machines. For machines—whether for the First or Fourth Industrial Revolution variety—downtime is a bug; for humans, downtime is a feature. The science is clear. And what it tells us is that there's simply no way you can make good decisions and achieve your world-changing ambitions while running on empty.
>
> Working 120-hour weeks doesn't leverage your unique qualities, it wastes them. You can't simply power through—that's just not how our bodies and our brains work. Nobody

knows better than you that we can't get to Mars by ignoring the laws of physics. Nor can we get where we want to go by ignoring scientific laws in our daily lives.[13]

Huffington explains that stress penalizes companies because it reduces productivity. She underlines another imbalance[14]: women who experience job-related stress have a 40 percent higher risk of heart disease and 60 percent greater risk of diabetes.

As a consequence, companies that want women—and all employees—to reach their full potential should seriously reconsider their workplace culture. It is an absolute necessity. This was confirmed by a McKinsey 2015 report[15] entitled "Diversity Matters." It shows that companies in the top quartile for gender diversity on their executive teams are 15 percent more likely to have above-average financial returns than those in the fourth quartile. In 2018, this number rose to 21 percent.

A greater presence of women in business will mean a brighter future for business as a whole. Each day that does not go in this direction is a day lost. The slowness of change in this regard is unacceptable. It's why Arianna Huffington, Oprah Winfrey, and thousands of other women, and men, have multiplied their calls to action. Winfrey focuses more on challenges in private life, for example, by combatting violence against women. Huffington focuses more on the sphere of business, by fighting for the accession of women to the boardroom. But their missions blend together. As the McKinsey Global Institute noted, "Gender equality at work is not achievable without gender equality in society."[16]

PART

FIVE

DISRUPTIVE SOCIAL PURPOSE

S ocial consciousness among business leaders is not new.

I begin this part on corporate social responsibility (CSR) by paying tribute to Sarah Breedlove, better known as Madam C. J. Walker. In her time she was the wealthiest African-American woman and the "nation's first self-made female millionaire."[1] She was also one of the first entrepreneurs in America to make social purpose and business work together. After having fought for civil rights for Blacks all her life, she donated a large part of her fortune to charity upon her death in 1919.

She was born in 1867, a few years after Abraham Lincoln issued the Emancipation Proclamation. Her parents were former cotton plantation slaves, and Breedlove started with absolutely nothing—and with the odds stacked against her. Orphaned at the age of 7, married at 14, and widowed with a daughter at 20, she worked long and hard for a pittance, up until 1905. That year, starting from scratch, she created the C. J. Walker Manufacturing Company, through which she developed and sold her own line of hair care products.

Her star products included a hair lotion and a pomade made from extracts of traditional African herbs. Her life took her way beyond her tough childhood and challenging early life, and she became a legendary entrepreneur and philanthropist. At the National Negro Business League Convention in July 1912, she declared, "I am a woman who came from the cotton fields of the South. I was promoted from there to the washtub. Then I was promoted to the cook kitchen. And from there I promoted myself into the business of manufacturing hair goods and preparations. . . . I have built my own factory on my own ground."[2]

Her products gradually became more and more successful. Then, in 1920, Josephine Baker, the famous American-born French entertainer, began using them, and Breedlove's success became international. Today, you can still find products with the Madam C. J. Walker label in luxury cosmetics outlets like Sephora.

Madam C. J. Walker was a pioneer in three domains: peer-to-peer marketing, community marketing, and cause marketing.

The enterprise she founded counted a sales force of up to 3,000 employees, whose job was to present the Walker System of Beauty Culture door to door. The role of these Walker Agents"[3] was not just to sell products, but also to promote Madam C. J. Walker's philosophy of "cleanliness and loveliness,"[4] which consisted of educating people in the community about hygiene, personal pride, and the value of good appearance. Breedlove also owned several beauty salons throughout New York City. Clients were encouraged to promote the products to other potential clients. Over 25,000 of them eventually became agents for the brand. Madam C. J. Walker called them, back then, her "Beauty Culturists."[5]

She maintained very close ties with the African-American community and with the multitude of parish church micro-communities in particular. She allowed thousands of black workers to achieve financial emancipation and she became both a role model and spokesperson for the black community.

More than a century before the expression was first employed, she became an authentic activist CEO. She fought with all her strength against the poor treatment of Blacks, and played an active role at the Negro Silent Protest Parade in 1917. She financed campaigns pushing for legislation to protect the rights of Blacks. She actively supported a great number of associations and organizations, such as the National Association for the Advancement of Colored People, serving the African-American community. She founded philanthropies, donated homes to the elderly, and funded orphanages. And 100 years before Warren Buffet, Bill Gates, or Mark Zuckerberg chose to donate a large part of their fortunes to philanthropic organizations, she had decided to bequeath two-thirds of her wealth[6] to charities that helped the Black community and people of color throughout the country.

The subject of corporate social responsibility has always generated a considerable body of literature. It goes all the way back to the Industrial Revolution, a time when observers accused the factory system as being the source of numerous social problems, including poverty, labor unrest, illiteracy, child labor, and the proliferation of slums. This gave birth to what was called the "welfare movement."

In the century since Breedlove's time, the perception of corporate social responsibility has never ceased to evolve. It has also expanded. At first, philanthropy manifested itself exclusively through charitable contributions. Then came the era of giving back, which saw firms and individuals returning to society part of what they had taken on their paths to success. Most companies now demonstrate their commitment to compensating any negative impact they may have on the world. The cumulative effect of their efforts is having a great influence on society, culture, and the environment. In a world where most governments' resources are stagnating, the private sector can and must help support public authorities. Today, of the 100 leading economic entities, 69 are corporations and 31 states.[7]

Younger generations are lucid about what governments are actually in a position to accomplish, so they expect more from business. A 2015 Nielsen report[8] revealed that the percentage of global consumers willing to pay higher prices for sustainable goods had grown by 11 points in one year, from 55 percent in 2014 to 66 percent in 2015. And among millennials, the number shifted by a staggering 23 points, from 50 percent to 73 percent. This study leads us to believe that consumer-goods brands that are committed to sustainability will end up overtaking those that are not.

Grinnell College, in Iowa, traditionally directs its research and publications toward the subject of social justice. Over 60 years ago, its president at the time, Howard Bowen, was the first to use the expression "corporate social responsibility."[9] He defined the social obligation of businessmen to concern themselves with the values and expectations of society. As explained one of his colleagues, "[Bowen] extended the domain of moral responsibility into the territory of corporate capitalism."[10] Since then, the concept has continued to strengthen and spread. Today, chief sustainability officers, who look after the triple bottom line— financial, environmental, and social—report directly to CEOs in companies everywhere.

The business world has become more aware of the win/ win opportunity at hand, for both the company and for society, through the combining of business and social responsibility. Unilever's Chief Marketing and Communications Officer, Keith Weed, describes himself as a firm believer in business ability to be "a force for good."[11]

But this is not yet the case for everyone. Some executives still remain somewhat skeptical. Others are simply not receptive to the idea. They often hide behind Milton Friedman's famous affirmation in a 1970 *New York Times* article: "The social responsibility of business is to increase its profit."[12] This statement is based on the idea that the company is already contributing its share to society through the salaries and the taxes it pays. According to Milton Friedman, it is precisely because the company seeks to maximize its profits that it can pay consequential amounts in taxes. With these funds, governments can finance their efforts in the fields of society and environment. It's up to all to respect their particular role. The argument appears irrefutable, but Friedman's supporters and critics have been arguing about it for 50 years.

Michael Porter, in a paper[13] co-authored with Mark Kramer in 2011, brings arguments that go beyond this ongoing debate. Central to their ideas is the concept of "shared value creation" (SVC), which is progressively replacing that of CSR among experts and specialists on the subject. There already exists a plethora of publications comparing CSR and SVC. According to Porter, the shared value creation concept focuses on the idea that doing good in the end also drives "productivity growth."[14] To do so, he exhorts companies to look for the right kind of profit, profit that creates rather than reduces social benefits. It's no longer a case of choosing between two types of priorities, as if privileging one would necessarily be to the detriment of the other.

With SVC, environmental, cultural, and societal activities are no longer peripheral concerns for companies. Social responsibility has become mainstream. It is not something that companies begin to think about after they have made their money, but rather that they contemplate upstream by asking *how* that money should be made in the first place.

CSR is a vast subject and companies address it in many different ways. I will describe very briefly some examples before concentrating on three major multinationals making a big impact.

First, I would like to say a few words about those firms that built their business models on CSR from the outset. This includes one-for-one companies like Toms or Warby Parker. The first gives away a pair of shoes, the other a pair of eyeglasses, to needy people in poor countries each time a customer from a wealthy country buys a pair. These enterprises are proof that CSR can be a core business driver. The CEO of Toms, Blake Mycoskie, goes as far as to assert "giving helps generate revenue."[15]

Second, I wish to mention companies that concentrate a major part of their activities on social purpose, but not in the one-to-one way. I'm thinking here of organizations like the Unreasonable Group, Care.com, and Make.org. The cumulative effect of their activities helps to make the world a better place, for the benefit of all.

Third, I would like to acknowledge the great foundations, such as that of Bill and Melinda Gates, which allocates up to $4 billion every year to multiple causes. They can never receive enough praise.

We are living in a world of social responsibility that is multifaceted, generous, and inventive. Each day sees the birth of promising new ideas and initiatives, such as those inspired by the three multinationals that I chose to concentrate on in the following chapters. Two are from the old economy and one is from the new: Unilever, Danone, and Salesforce. None of these companies were born from CSR, and yet, it has become central to all of their activities. Unilever, under the leadership of Paul Polman, is without doubt the firm that has deployed CSR in the most explicit and comprehensive way. Danone, a company that has been pioneering social responsibility since 1970, and whose current CEO, Emmanuel Faber, is committed more than ever to making social issues and business work hand in hand. Finally, I will discuss Salesforce, whose co-founder Marc Benioff has become the standard bearer for CSR in the business world.

Social responsibility has become so much part of these three corporations that I cannot imagine them ever going back. Their employees, their clients, their suppliers, and their shareholders would simply not understand.

CHAPTER 18

PAUL POLMAN

ON COMPLETE CSR AND CORPORATE ACTIVISM

At the beginning of 2009, on one of his first days as head of Unilever, Paul Polman informed the financial world that he would no longer be giving earnings forecasts to the firm's investors. He likes to say that he felt empowered to do this right away because "the day they hire you, they are not going to fire you."[1]

Well aware of the mixed reactions this bold move would create among potential investors, he explained that his priority was now the creation of long-term value. And he thought that the only possible path to achieve this was to put social purpose at the heart of his enterprise.

A Force for Good

Polman is the very example of the chief executive convinced of the soundness of shared value creation. No one has been more determined than he has been in putting into place what has become an extremely comprehensive CSR program—perhaps the most far-reaching to have ever been undertaken by a large corporation. He has always believed in the idea that looking after the least fortunate and protecting the planet were equal parts business opportunity and moral obligation. For him, it's impossible to build a strong, sustainable business in a world of increasing inequality, poverty, and climate change.

His program is called the Unilever Sustainable Living Plan. It is multifaceted, and founded on three overarching objectives: to improve the health and well-being of over one billion people, to halve the impact his company and its supply chain have on the environment, and to upgrade the living conditions of hundreds of millions of people. This plan has led the company to respond to many different environmental issues, such as greenhouse-gas emissions, water preservation, waste treatment, and sustainable supplies, and has resulted in Unilever's confronting social topics such as working conditions, equity in the workplace, gender equality, health, and education. The company implements hundreds of different initiatives every year on all these key subjects, in the countries in which it operates, in each of the sectors it occupies, and for each of its different brands.

The Sustainable Living Plan replies to a dual objective: to minimize Unilever's negative impact, while at the same time maximizing its positive one. By minimizing, the company intends to repair some of the damage it has caused, like many companies around the world, in the normal course of business. By maximizing, Unilever means developing innovative social policies that have a long-term beneficial impact on society.

Polman's bold strategy has paid off financially. The Unilever Sustainable Living Plan he launched in 2010 has been a great success, despite the initial doubt of critics and investors. The Plan proved that there does not have to be a trade-off between sustainability and profitable growth. The numbers have clearly proven him right. In nine years, Unilever's sales have increased on average at twice the rate of the market. They delivered a 290 percent return on investment to shareholders, much higher than the average overall stock market returns. Polman has thus provided a formal rebuttal to those who thought that a responsible business model could not serve long-term shareholder value. It should be added that Unilever's shareholders also remain with the company much longer than the average, with an unheard of 70 percent staying seven years or more.

After nearly 10 years at the head of Unilever, Polman is now handing the reins to his successor. This book is dedicated to those who will leave their mark in the business world in a way that goes beyond the boundaries of their own companies; in this, Polman will occupy a special place. Better than anyone, he represents what is expected of a great business leader, and in particular by millennials, who will soon make up 50 percent[2] of the workforce. People want business leaders to be actively concerned about the state of the world.

Investors needed to be convinced and consumers also had to be persuaded to change their behavior. The way in which products are used can actually directly reduce their negative impact on the environment. The company measured[3] the environmental footprints of 2,000 of its different products. It discovered that 68 percent of its greenhouse-gas emissions occurred after the products were in the hands of the end user. Ordinary but energy-intensive activities, like boiling water to make the tea or doing the laundry, are how these emissions are created.

This led Polman to draw up a list of what he calls The Five Levers for Change. Often, people don't know how they should behave and why. They are more likely to act if it's easy for them, but not if it requires extra effort. Once they have changed their behavior, it is important to find ways to help them maintain their good new habits over time. To help other businesses educate their consumers, Unilever's CEO suggested that companies use these five levers: "make it understood, make it easy, make it desirable, make it rewarding, and make it a habit."[4] The goal is to make good behavior commonplace.

Polman is an environmental evangelist. For him, business is part of the solution, not of the problem. Sustainability is a powerful business driver; it guarantees the longevity of business as well as the future of our planet. This belief is also the credo of the Business & Sustainable Development Commission, which was launched in 2016 and of which Polman is a co-founder. The aim of this commission is to push industry leaders around the world to embrace the UN 2030 Sustainability Development Goals agenda and to incorporate it as a key driver for their business strategies, innovation, and investment decisions. Polman cites the conclusions of the prospective study carried out by the commission: "If we help harness markets—and all the financial, human and innovation capital they represent—to deliver the world we want, it comes with a minimum $12 trillion opportunity and the creation of 380 million more jobs. It's worth going for."[5]

Unilever has demonstrated that it is in businesses' best interests to drive societal change. And it would appear that many others agree. One can, for instance, cite projects such as Ikea's People & Planet, Nissan's Blue Citizenship, HP's Living Progress, or McDonald's Scale for Good.

Despite Polman's strong commitment, not all of Unilever's brands have embraced the sustainable plan in the same way. It depends on each brand's profile and on the level of buy-in of its leader. However, a key learning has emerged from the company's observations: The most purpose-driven brands, such as Ben & Jerry's, Dove, or Hellman's are also the most profitable. In terms of sales, in 2017, Unilever's 26 Sustainable Living brands grew 46 percent faster than the rest of its business. And they delivered 70 percent of the overall growth in turnover.

This powerful result is even more significant than it may at first appear. Unilever is showing the way. It is proving to the world that a company can be a force both for growth and for good. We should be reassured by the fact that it is succeeding. A journalist from the *Economist* puts it this way, "If Unilever cannot make the sustainability idea pay—with its deep pockets, long corporate history and determined boss—then perhaps no other firm can."[6]

CEO Activism

Today, business leaders no longer need journalists when they want to publicly voice their opinions. They have Twitter, which allows Polman, and many others, to express their thoughts not just on business or economic subjects, but also on the problems of society.

Polman follows in the footsteps of Marilyn Carlson Nelson, co-owner of Carlson Travel, who in 2004 took a stand against human trafficking. It's widely held that she opened the way back then to what we now call CEO activism.

Increasingly, corporate leaders are entering into public debate on topics that up until now were considered the sole domain of politicians. They are taking positions on social issues that have no direct link with their businesses. For example, they can make their opinions known on a local level regarding proposed state legislation that goes against the values they defend. Think of the indignation of Howard Schultz of Starbucks, Tim Cook of Apple, or Dan Schumann of PayPal on legislation planned by the states of Georgia, North Carolina, or Indiana that would have negatively impacted gender equality. At a federal level, many CEOs have also reacted vigorously against the Trump administration's new anti-immigration plan, as well as to the withdrawal of the United States from the 2015 Paris Agreement on climate change.

In the last few years, more and more company heads have been exposing their points of view on the subjects that stir society today: gender equality, health coverage, climate change, income fairness, immigration, and, in general, anything relating to discrimination. Each time, the same process takes place. Chief executives relay their messages via social networks. Then, digital audiences support or contest them, which creates a buzz that is then picked up by the media.

A Weber Shandwick survey[7] shows that 51 percent of consumers are more likely to buy from a company whose chief executive is engaged in public debate on important societal subjects. A majority of employees say that their loyalty to their company is influenced by whether or not their chief executive is prepared to speak out on crucial issues. The millennials' generation, which possesses an acute sense of political consciousness, believes that business leaders are more likely to make things happen than politicians who, in their view, have already demonstrated their incapacity to act on a number of important issues.

The activism movement has become so large that there are now concerns about the "cost of silence."[8] Leaders who do not appear to be engaged on burning social issues relevant to their companies are at risk of consumer boycotts or internal employee petitions. CEO activism has rapidly taken on a new dimension.

I mentioned earlier some of those activist CEOs who stood up against the new American immigration policies. Let me cite now another, Hamdi Ulukaya, who adopted a courageous and unusual approach. He's the founder and CEO of the multi-billion-dollar yogurt company Chobani. In less than two decades he has been able to hoist his company to the ranks of Dannon and General Mills in the United States. He owes his meteoric success to a new kind of business leadership he installed, "one that fuses competitiveness with an unusually strong sense of compassion."[9] He was featured on the cover of *Fast Company* with the headline: "Immigrant. CEO. Billionaire." The subtitle was "How Chobani founder Hamdi Ulukaya is winning America's culture war."[10]

Chobani's employees come from over 15 different countries. Almost one in three is an immigrant. The company actually employs more than 400 refugees. And Ulukaya has given 10 percent of Chobani's equity to its workers. All this doesn't stop him from being very tough in business, and even feared by his competitors. He has a reputation for moving very fast, while at the same time maintaining an extraordinary sense of detail. He is clearly at the dawn of creating a food giant. Not a bad performance for a guy who, in his early years in Turkey, had a clearly anti-capitalist spirit. His stance has been criticized by the most rigid U.S. political leaders when it comes to immigration, but this has not made him budge an inch. On the subject of helping others, he says, "I don't want more, I just want to do more."[11]

Increasingly, this will be the case for those leaders driven to be true forces for good. Apart from the inevitable and thorny issues they must face internally, such as gender equality, salary fairness, and religious expression in the workplace, chief executives will also have to deal with those dramatic topics that will influence the future of humanity as a whole. We all know that our world is going through a very difficult time, and are aware of the absolute necessity to help the most fragile, those whose voices are not heard. Chief executives, whose voices do carry, know they no longer have the right to stay silent. It's not just a moral obligation, but also an opportunity for their business. People who are forgotten today, and see no cynicism in this, may be customers tomorrow.

Coming back to Polman, he evolved naturally into this global trend. He also remained realistic and knew that most heads of industry are still far from being convinced that it is in their interest to serve society as a whole. This is why he spent so much of his time fighting for his convictions. Instead of talking to the press about his company's results, he spoke as often as possible about the need to work toward a better world. That was not something all investors wanted to hear.

Yet, things started to change when the financial community actually began to share his point of view. In this sector, Black-Rock has led the way. BlackRock is the world's largest investor and manages no less than $6 trillion. Its CEO, Larry Fink, sent a letter in January 2018 to the heads of the largest public companies, stating, somewhat unexpectedly, "Society is demanding that companies, both public or private, serve a social purpose. To prosper over time, every company must not only deliver financial performance, but also show how it makes a positive contribution to society."[12]

This stance was astonishing for many. BlackRock had generally invested in companies that followed the Friedman theory, whereby their only duty was to generate more profit. Fink decided that his company would no longer be a passive investor, but that it would now take into account the triple bottom line in the companies in which it invests. BlackRock will evaluate prospective investments on three criteria: their financial performance, their environmental impact, and their social commitment. No more non-engagement.

Fink is now convinced that profit and purpose can work together—or rather that they *should* work together. Since, as *The New York Times* reported, "It's worth noting he's not playing down the importance of profits and while it's a subtle point, he believes that having a social purpose is inextricably linked to a company's ability to maintain its profits."[13] Like a growing number of chief executives, he feels that the long-term survival of business itself is at stake. For him, if a company doesn't embrace social purpose, "it will ultimately lose the license to operate from key stakeholders."[14]

I hope that his letter will be a turning point. It would seem so. When BlackRock talks, everyone listens.

CHAPTER 19

EMMANUEL FABER

ON SOCIAL PURPOSE AND THE BOTTOM OF THE PYRAMID

D anone is a French multinational food conglomerate. In America, its products are branded Dannon. They sell yogurts and mineral waters, as well as products for infant and medical nutrition. Its sales reached €24.7 billion in 2017 and its market capitalization was €42.1 billion at the end of 2018.

Antoine Riboud was chairman and CEO of the company from 1965 to 1996, and left his mark on the business world with his avant-garde thinking, in particular in terms of environmental and social affairs. In France, he remains one of the most charismatic bosses of his time.

In 1972, the remarkable speech he gave in Marseilles was a milestone in his career. Fifteen years before Norway's former prime minister, Gro Harlem Brundtland, who was at the time President of the UN World Commission on Environment and

Development, laid the foundations of sustainable development, Riboud had been promoting the idea inside his company. In the early 1970s, he insisted on including societal concerns in corporate strategies. He launched the "double project,"[1] with both a social and economic dimension that is still felt in the heart of the company. His heritage is, above all, illustrated through its social breadth.

Since then, semantics have evolved. Corporate language has changed, but today's ideas have been around for some time. It was inconceivable for Riboud that progress should leave behind workers who, in his own words, "were numerous to benefit insufficiently from the fruits of growth."[2] He thought that companies' responsibilities did not end at the doorstep of their offices or factories. He was convinced that their actions had repercussions on local communities, impacting the life of each citizen. In Marseilles, he concluded his speech in these terms: "Lead our companies with our hearts as well as our heads, and don't forget that if the world's energy resources are limited, those of man are infinite, if they feel motivated."[3]

Nearly 50 years later, Emmanuel Faber, the current CEO of Danone, took up the torch, and has shown himself to be a worthy successor of Riboud. As a business philosopher and humanist, Emmanuel Faber distinguishes himself with his far-reaching ideas. These open up unexplored and promising paths, but they are also disturbing for some people, including some shareholders and investors. Emmanuel Faber is a leader who could be described as dissident because of his unique vision of the company, a vision that is in many ways disruptive.

Side Roads

Chemins de Traverse (in English *Side Roads*) is the title of a book he published in 2011. In it, he pleads that another economic model is possible. His ideas are bold, but his feet are firmly planted on the ground.

Passionate about social justice, he rejects the notion of the company with no other mission than maximizing shareholder value. Evoking a world seen through financial eyes, he speaks of "lobotomized, dehumanized thinking."[4] He castigates the dictatorship of numbers and rebels against the preeminence given to the rational. He considers the rational as "the realm of deduction," and argues that "deduction creates nothing." For him, "It is intuition that creates new things."[5] Without it, nothing would be possible.

Emmanuel Faber is also a critic of management jargon, which he considers too narrow and restricting. This vocabulary seems to him all the more penalizing since it influences the thinking of the leaders of the world, preventing them access to another conception of the economic sphere. He goes so far as to attribute a social responsibility to globalization, which would lead to an equitable sharing of the work, the natural resources, and the know-how of the planet. "The challenge of globalization is to know what social role it can and must play,"[6] he says.

Emmanuel Faber does not in any way deny his obligations to Danone's shareholders, but at the same time, he stresses his obligations to his employees. "In a large publicly traded company, no shareholder has taken the same personal risk to the company as one of its employees. None of them has used their salary to obtain a loan to buy a house near the factory, nor to raise their family in this small town with its social structure of which Danone is a part. This obligation therefore entails an even stronger responsibility, more complex for employees than for shareholders. It is a fact." He goes on to say that "we have opposed the social and the economic, but they are the two facets of one and the same reality. The border between the two goes to the very heart of our consciousness, nowhere else."[7]

Danone has always believed that the well-being of society starts with health. From the beginning, the company placed it at the center of its concerns. In the 1920s, Danone products were exclusively available through pharmacies. In the late 1960s, when its products were being sold in supermarkets, the company had launched a multitude of gourmet desserts, which risked diluting its health-related image. That's why in the mid-1980s, its management made the decision to refocus on health. At that time, I recommended creating an institute dedicated to the pursuit of a deeper understanding of the relationship between food and health. The Danone Institute for Health was born. It devoted itself to major public health topics such as obesity, aging, and the strengthening of the immune system. The Institute funded the work of doctors, scientists, and nutritionists. Our agency later conceived an advertising campaign to publicize the Institute's activities. This campaign took the theme of what Hippocrates had recommended, to make food our first medicine. It was signed with a simple line explaining Danone's commitment to health: "*Danone, entreprendre pour la santé.*"

For Danone, food is anything but a commodity. It is much more than just a consumer product. With the "One Planet, One Health"[8] plan, Faber advocates equal health for all. Over and above the sale of healthy products, the company's mission is to promote better eating habits. The road ahead to achieve this goal is long and arduous. Not only do the inhabitants of our planet have unbalanced diets, but also the entire food chain has been degraded, starting with the simplest of products. According to a study conducted by Canadian professors and published in *L'Obs* magazine[9], an apple now contains 100 times less vitamin C and an orange 20 times less vitamin A than they did in 1950. This was one of the reasons Faber wanted Danone to buy WhiteWave Foods, the American champion of bio and vegetable proteins, thus positioning Danone in the consumption segment of tomorrow. "We have bought a part of the future,"[10] he said at the time of the acquisition.

This is all forward-looking and highly responsible, and yet it does not spare Danone from being the target of criticism. For instance, the company is often attacked for pushing its powdered infant formula, while many health organizations promote breastfeeding. And then, as a world leader in mineral water, Danone produces a lot of plastic bottles. On certain subjects, the company could be accused of being a bit ambivalent. As Unilever's Paul Polman said, inventing innovative social policies is not enough. You also have to actively reduce the negative impact of what you do. It's hard to be totally exemplary from one day to the next.

Despite these challenges, Faber's ambition is for Danone to become a B-corporation ("B" for "benefit"), commonly known as a B-corp. This is a new kind of business entity that balances purpose and profit, and that is legally required to generate social and environmental advantages in order to trade. The Danone Group has entities in the United States, Canada, Spain, the United Kingdom, France, and Argentina that have already obtained this difficult certified B-corp status. They represent 30 percent of the group's turnover. The B-Lab certifying body is very rigorous. So far, certification had only been granted to small or medium-sized companies. The group set itself the goal of becoming the first multinational to be totally B-Corp.

The Bottom of the Pyramid

The expression "bottom of the pyramid"[11] was used some 20 years ago by C. K. Pralahad to define the four billion people living on less than $1,500 a year. If we can allow ourselves to describe people who have access to almost nothing as a market, the bottom of the pyramid represents the largest untapped potential market in the world.

To reach these disadvantaged populations, which still account for two-thirds of our planet's inhabitants, we must develop products that cost less than a dollar to buy. It's only by adapting products to the needs and means of the poorest that poverty can be really reduced. Everything then becomes a question of scale. Selling very large volumes can offset fixed costs, in order to combat poverty while still making a profit.

Companies such as Procter & Gamble and Unilever are thus looking for ways to make household products affordable for the poorest. What these corporations seek to do is to bring into our consumer society that part of the world's population currently excluded from it. This is in their long-term business interest.

Danone's directors are not being left out of this. They have multiplied their initiatives in this direction. This is what first led the company to approach Muhammad Yunus, the pioneer of microcredit. He has helped millions of workers in the southern hemisphere to create their own microenterprises and achieve a form of financial independence. Grameen Danone Foods was born in 2006 as a result of this encounter, and became the world's first purpose-designed multinational social business. In a social enterprise, shareholders recover their initial investment after a given period of time, but do not receive any dividends. It may well be driven by philanthropic considerations, but it must still function as a business. A social enterprise needs to develop and grow to cover its operating costs, whereas a charity relies exclusively on donations.

Grameen Danone Foods is one such "no-dividend"[12] business. In Bangladesh, it launched the Shokti Doi, a yogurt enriched with the highest levels of minerals and vitamins ever attained. This nutritionist-developed yogurt covers 30 percent of a child's daily nutrient requirements for the modest sum of 6 taka[13], or 0.07 cents. This also allowed the company to kill three birds with one stone. First, it has helped reduce poverty in the countryside by working hand in hand with farmers. Second, in factories, by recruiting a maximum number of people from the local community. Finally, on the ground, by creating 1,500 jobs and employing Shokti Ladies to distribute the products in villages. In 2006, Muhammad Yunus and Grameen Bank were awarded the Nobel Peace Prize. Later, *Fortune* magazine, at the time of the opening of a new Danone's Shokti Doi factory in Bangladesh, featured a cover story. The headline was "Saving the World with a Cup of Yogurt."[14]

Faber wanted to go even further. Using the momentum of the success of Grameen Danone Foods, he has injected life into a new initiative, Danone Communities. This is an incubator for micro-enterprises in poor countries, a network of social businesses, disposing of a budget of €70 million. Danone Communities is a way of financing and supporting social business projects aimed at reducing poverty and malnutrition. Believing in the concept, a third of Danone's own employees have chosen to invest in the different programs initiated by Danone Communities. These projects, all of them innovative, have thus been financed in countries where the economy is fragile. If successful, these experiences can be replicated in other countries.

A few years ago, the CEO of Danone managed to convince first his board, then 98 percent of the investors attending the annual shareholders' meeting, to draw on the company reserves an amount equal to 20 percent of the dividends that would be distributed to them that year. Faber's objective was to be able to protect the external labor pool in those regions where his offices and factories are located. Danone employs over 100,000 people worldwide, but five to seven times as many jobs are directly dependent on the group's activities. The idea was to invigorate the workforce where the company is present by investing in the local communities and, as Faber says, "to strengthen the capacity to grow of all the economic actors who live on the periphery of a multinational."[15]

For several decades, most multinationals assumed that the proportion of turnover contributed by international brands within their overall portfolio would be in constant progression. Until recently, Danone's management had expected Actimel's and Activia's cumulative sales to exceed 30 percent of the company's total revenue. This is no longer the case. Management is fully alerted to the recent and underlying disaffection toward international brands. For the past five years, all industries considered, local brands have been nibbling away at major international brands. This has happened in every region, at a rate of one half to one point of market share year after year. This trend echoes an analysis by *The Economist* on the weakening of the global company. The article, entitled "The Retreat of the Global Company,"[16] explained that the profits generated by 700 multinational companies worldwide have decreased by 25 percent since 2012, while those of local firms have increased by 2 percent.

For Faber, the conventional model adopted by the agro-food industry for the past 50 years, based on globalization to reduce costs, has reached its limits in today's social and environmental context, as well as on the economic front. His conclusion is unequivocal: "When obesity progresses, when the yield of agricultural land falls, when pollution climbs and when the agricultural world has more and more difficulty to live from its efforts, it is time to change the model."[17]

This explains Danone's decision to re-localize its production facilities and to promote local brands. In this way the company is looking to improve the biodiversity of eating habits and agricultural practices. That being said, these local brands that Danone supports are neither small nor old. Aqua, for example, is the leading brand of bottled mineral water in Indonesia, as is Font Vella in Spain. Mizone is the number-one vitamin drink in China. Milupa and Nutricia are both leaders in therapeutic food in Germany and Holland, respectively. As for WhiteWave Foods, the U.S. brand that Danone bought in 2017 for $12.5 billion, it was born less than a generation ago. For Faber, anchoring Danone's activities in each of the territories in which the company operates is fundamental, because food is cultural, social, and local. The company has now pivoted, placing its priority on local.

The ultimate vision of Danone's CEO, as he said himself, is to gradually "resynchronize the food chain"[18] to bring back together nature, agriculture, food, and nutrition. Social purpose and business purpose will then become one.

CHAPTER 20

MARC BENIOFF
AND SUZANNE DIBIANCA

ON SCALING UP PHILANTHROPY

When new employees arrive at Salesforce, they are shown their desk, given a computer, and fed some information about the daily life of the company. Then, after barely an hour, Salesforce sends them out to do a day of volunteering at a school, hospital, or homeless shelter. The company makes it immediately clear how much social purpose is at the heart of its activities. For Salesforce, it is a driving principle.

Salesforce is one of the fastest-growing enterprise software companies in the world. The leading provider of cloud-based customer relationship management software, Salesforce truly fueled the explosion of software as a service.

A Native Philanthropist

From the very beginning, when Salesforce employed only a few people in a San Francisco apartment, the idea of giving back was integrated into its business model. As then, it is based on three pillars, two of a commercial order, one charitable. First, the company decided to give free access to part of its software on the Internet, which was a completely new concept in 1999. Second, using another approach unprecedented at the time, Salesforce commercialized its software on a monthly subscription basis. It was the beginning of a period in the business-to-business segment, in which usage has taken precedence over ownership. Finally, in a third innovation, the company developed a new philanthropic model, which is simple, engaging, and capable of lasting over time.

When it was still in start-up mode, Salesforce invented the now famous 1–1–1 model. It has made philanthropy a pillar of its activities by donating 1 percent of its products, 1 percent of its equity, and 1 percent of its employees' time to charity. And to help ensure success, Marc Benioff created the Salesforce Foundation in the company's first year of existence, with Suzanne DiBianca at its head. Today, almost 20 years later, she is still the chief philanthropy officer of the company. It is common practice for firms to create their own foundation once they have made their name, when they think they have become sufficiently institutionalized, and therefore legitimate, to do so. But for Benioff, the time felt right after only a few months.

Salesforce has since distributed more than $230 million in grants, provided more than 37,000 nonprofit and higher education institutions with access to enterprise-developed software, and invested around 3.2 million hours of its employees' time for community service.[1]

The Salesforce Foundation does not defend a single cause. To the contrary, a video on its website explains that the company works for a cleaner planet, fewer homeless people, less hunger, more jobs, reduced poverty, wildlife protection, increased literacy, productive workplace, healthier communities, veteran support, successful graduations, efficient disaster response, accessible resources, disease prevention, not to forget education, the company's explicit top priority. Conventional thinking might say that this list is too long, that Salesforce's initiatives are too diversified. Many philanthropy experts insist that efforts must be targeted. In other words, there must be a clear link between the business activity of the company and its charitable projects. Procter & Gamble, for example, has adopted this targeted approach, as we've seen, for its corporate social responsibility policy. Salesforce acts differently. The company supports its own employees in the charitable projects in which they are personally involved and, in this way, gives them more weight. Most often, Salesforce abounds the gifts made by its employees. This leads to pilots, experiments that, if successful, are then proposed to municipalities, states, or even federal policy makers, to be implemented on a larger scale. At the end of the video, a little girl says, "1%, when you count it up, it's actually a lot," followed by text on the screen that reads, "Give 1%. And watch great things happen."[2]

As Suzanne DiBianca stated recently: "We believe companies are the greatest platform for social change."[3]

There are many ways to explain the Salesforce approach. Here are a few: There is no distinction between the company's drive for growth and its social impact. Profit and purpose are not in conflict anymore. Corporate social responsibility is a driver to profitability. Running a company with close attention to its environmental and social impact is not an act of charity, but of self-interest. And last but not least, as Benioff himself says, "The business of business is improving the state of the world."[4]

A company that wants to be a force for good outside must be, as far as possible, close to exemplary inside. Benioff is committed. He has already taken a series of measures to move toward equality in four key areas: equal rights, equal pay, equal education, and equal opportunities. When he found out, to his great surprise, that there were wage differentials between men and women in his own company, he immediately released the $6 million needed to put things right.

The 1–1–1 model stands out for its simplicity, and fits perfectly into contemporary thinking. As we saw with Danone's Emmanuel Faber, CSR reflects corporate leaders' growing awareness of their responsibilities to all their stakeholders, including the communities where their businesses are located and where their employees live. Future generations want to see CEOs take on the problems of our society, to try to solve them, within the limits of their means, but with real determination. Benioff intends to meet millennials' expectations; he likes to say that even if he is not a millennial himself, he certainly has a millennial view of the world.

Like Faber, Polman, and a large number of other chief executives, who are neither skeptics nor cynical on these topics, Benioff demonstrates that doing good for society means doing good for his company. This view is shared by Jason Wicks in his book *The Price of Profit*: "Sort of paradoxically, for a firm to maximize profit, they will actually have to start caring about other things than profit."[5]

Pledge 1%

The success of his 1–1–1 philanthropic model led Benioff to ask himself these questions: What if other companies, especially start-ups, adopted the same model? What if they mirrored what Salesforce achieved? What if other companies shared the same culture of giving back?

In 2014, he spun off the Salesforce 1–1–1 initiative as Pledge 1%. He began by evangelizing start-ups, and later established companies, that the conventional approach using grants is much less efficient than the Salesforce way. The foundation created "Share the Model,"[6] a program designed to encourage other companies to embrace his integrated philanthropic approach. Benioff definitely wants to help other companies to also have a real impact on the world.

With its three distinct chapters—product, equity, people—Pledge 1% is a great framework for corporate leaders who do not yet have any experience in corporate social responsibility. It demonstrates, as DiBianca has said, that "your technology, your products, and your time are just as valuable as the dollars you can give away."[7] Often, heads of companies do not know where to start, which cause to choose, with which social partners to associate, and which funding method to use. When a company decides to adopt the 1–1–1 model, a member of the foundation contacts its management. The foundation guides the company, provides advice, gives tools, offers resources, and shares best practices. It connects new members with firms that have already successfully implemented the program. A community of Pledge 1% companies has thus emerged. There are now more than 5,000 around the world that have joined the movement. By exporting Salesforce's disruptive social purpose model, Benioff and DiBianca have given new energy to corporate philanthropy,

allowing it to expand to unheard-of levels. Thousands of benefi-
ciaries are able to testify of its success.

In this way, the private sector comes to the rescue of the
public sector. As we know, it has become common these days to
point out the helplessness of state authorities. They are burdened
by debt, their leaders are focused on the short term, and their
actions are restricted by their national borders. Meanwhile, the
stakes themselves are borderless, global. For their part, NGOs,
whose cumulative action is considerable, are sorely lacking in the
means to scale up their philanthropic actions. In such a context,
the contribution of business is vital. We now refer to Capitalism
2.0, a world where the very first question that you would ask
about a company would be about the contribution it makes to
society at large.

For Polman, Faber, and Benioff, we have reached a point of
no return. They have demonstrated their unwavering commitment, but they are not blind to the fact that their efforts have
limits. They know that while the business world's commitment
is essential, business alone cannot solve the planet's problems.
That's why they believe it has become imperative for all change
agents to unite, be they international institutions, governments,
companies, foundations, NGOs, or social businesses. Only if
they act in concert, will they be able to start to really repair the
world.

To conclude this part, I submit a remark made by Ban
Ki-moon, the former Secretary-General of the United Nations:
"We are the first generation that can put an end to poverty and
we are the last generation that can put an end to climate change."[8]

It is a heavy responsibility. We owe it to our children not to
fail. And the world of business has an undeniably important role
to play. As we've seen, this is in its best interest, and in the long

term even vital for its survival. It is therefore promising to see that more and more chief executives are becoming convinced. They consider philanthropy as a sound business practice. They see altruism as a way to create value. They believe that social purpose is a factor for growth.

Conclusion
Disruption Ahead

The period we live in is full of peril, but also full of great promise. It is a time in which thousands of inventions are just waiting to be discovered. The prospects are immense. Bioscience will allow us to live longer, artificial intelligence to multiply our creativity, renewable energy to meet the climate challenge. The condition is that we must learn how to master them. As is often the case in our history, there is concomitance between the appearance of a problem and the emergence of a solution. The Internet was born exactly when the world needed it. Data is now revolutionizing the future of healthcare. One day soon, we may find a way to extract greenhouse-gas emissions from the atmosphere on a major scale. We have entered a fecund period at all levels.

But this promise will not be realized automatically. To construct our collective future, broad change is vital. We must innovate in all directions. We will need to employ great imagination, and to think and act creatively. For each one of us, for the companies we work for, and for the world we live in, we will need disruption—everyday and everywhere.

This is why I wanted to celebrate all those men and women who have most impressed me with their disruptive leadership. It is encouraging to know that behind these great leaders, there are great companies. And that inside them, there is a real desire to transform things. This change can be accomplished by inventing as-yet-unheard-of solutions. By disrupting. It will be for the better, and give the word *disruption* the true meaning we intend it to have, a positive one.

So, to all those mentioned here, allow me to say again, *Thank you for disrupting.* I expect that in the coming years they will be joined by many other disruptive entrepreneurs, businessmen and businesswomen, or everyday citizens. People who will bring us radically innovative approaches, and help us take on the issues facing our world.

I also believe in the ability of each individual to be disruptive, imaginative, and entrepreneurial. We must—and this is one of the great challenges of our time—become capable of liberating the creative potential that lies within each of us.

As Gandhi said, "Be the change you want to see in the world." Whatever our activity, whatever our level of influence in the place where we work, it is up to us to not shy away, not leave to others the collective responsibility of making change happen. Each of us should, to the measure of his or her possibilities, become personally invested.

All of us must give life to, and let grow, what inside of us is most disruptive.

Acknowledgments

I would like to thank Pamela Tamby, my assistant of more than 10 years, and Nicholas Baum, a business partner and long-time friend. They worked tirelessly back and forth between the English and French versions of this book. At the end of the day, they had a great influence, not only on its form, but also on the content. Without them, this book would not be what it is.

My appreciation goes to Troy Ruhanen, Denis Streiff, Elaine Stein, Guillaume Pannaud, Nicolas Bordas, Jean-Marie Prénaud, Jean-David Sichel, Vincent Garel, Antoine Lesec, and Kou Yang for their unwavering support.

I would like to especially thank Christina Verigan for the quality of her work and for her invaluable contribution.

Last, but not least, I would also like to express my gratitude to Richard Narramore, my editor at John Wiley & Sons, for his advice, and his colleagues—Jocelyn Kwiatkowski, Peter Knox, Vicki Adang, and Victoria Anllo—for their precious help in preparing the book and its launch.

Notes

Introduction: Thank You for Disrupting

1. Upbin, Bruce (September 18, 2012), "Talking Philanthropy with Marc Benioff." *Forbes*.
2. Conversation with Zhang Ruimin by Knowledge@Wharton. "For Haier's Zhang Ruimin, success means creating the future." Retrieved from knowledge.wharton.upenn.edu, April 20, 2018.

Chapter 1: Steve Jobs

1. The Telegraph. (October 7, 2011). "Steve Jobs leaves behind product legacy that will last for years," *Telegraph*.
2. Balakrishnan, Anita (October 3, 2016). "Why Apple CEO Tim Cook doesn't ask, 'What would Steve Jobs do?" CNBC.com.
3. Stabiner, Karen (1993). *Inventing Desire: Inside Chiat/ Day: The Hottest Shop, the Coolest Players, the Big Business of Advertising*. New York: Simon & Schuster.

4. 1984 Apple Inc. Super Bowl commercial. Video available at https://www.youtube.com/watch?v=cDDzGr80KSY (accessed on January 10, 2019).

5. Carr, Austin (March 2017). "11-16 Alibaba, Tencent, Xiaomi, BBK Electronics, Huawei, Dalian Wanda for ramping up the pace for the world," *Fast Company*, issue 213, 48.

6. Gibson, Rowan (2015). *The Four Lenses of Innovation: A Power Tool for Creative Thinking.* Hoboken, NJ: John Wiley & Sons.

7. Cheney, Steve (August 18, 2013). "1980: Steve Jobs on Hardware Software Convergence," SteveCheney.com. Available at http://stevecheney.com/1980-steve-jobs-on-hardware-software-convergence (accessed December 17, 2018).

8. Gapper, John (January 11, 2017). "Steve Jobs' legacy is the omniscient tech company," *Financial Times*.

9. Brown, Tim and Roger Martin (September 2015). "Design for Action. How to use design thinking to make great things actually happen," *Harvard Business Review* 93(09), 57–64.

10. Cohen, Peter (May 22, 2015). "Saying no to 1,000 things," iMore.com. Available at: https://www.imore.com/saying-no-1000-things (accessed December 17, 2018).

11. Jobs, Steve (May 25, 1998) in an interview to *Bloomberg BusinessWeek*.

12. Steve Jobs' Commencement Address at Standford University (June 12, 2005). Available at https://news.stanford.edu/2005/06/14/jobs-061505/ (accessed December 17, 2018).

13. DNews (October 12, 2011). "Steve Jobs: Dents in the Universe." https://www.seeker.com/steve-jobs-dents-in-the-universe-1765465298.html (accessed December 17, 2018).

14. Sculley, John (Bloomberg TV, October 14, 2010). Quoted in a documentary series "Bloomberg Game Changers: Steve Jobs."

Chapter 2: Jeff Bezos

1. Bezos, Jeff (April 18, 2018). "2017 Letter to Shareholders." Available at https://blog.aboutamazon.com/company-news/2017-letter-to-shareholders (accessed December 18, 2018).
2. Hyken, Shep (July 22, 2018). "Amazon: The most convenient store on the planet," Forbes.com.
3. Bezos, Jeff (April 17, 2017). "2016 Letter to Shareholders." Available at https://blog.aboutamazon.com/company-news/2016-letter-to-shareholders (accessed December 18, 2018).
4. D'Onfro, Jillian (December 2, 2014). "Jeff Bezos: Why it won't matter if the Fire Phone flops," BusinessInsider.com.
5. Kim, Eugene (May 28, 2016). "How Amazon CEO Jeff Bezos has inspired people to change the way they think about failure," BusinessInsider.com.
6. Ibid.
7. Lashinsky, Adam (November 16, 2012). "Amazon's Jeff Bezos: the ultimate disrupter," Fortune website.
8. Salter, Chuck (February 6, 2009). "Kindle 2 preview: Jeff Bezos on why Amazon works backwards," Fast Company website.
9. McKendrick, Joe (February 13, 2016). "Prediction: every business will be a Cloud or digital platform provider, soon," Forbes.com Accenture 2016 Technology Vision report available at https://www.accenture.com/us-en/insight-digital-platform-economy.
10. Jeff Immelt's interview with Huijgen, Annelot and Ivan Letessier (June 15, 2016). "General Electric à l'offensive dans l'Internet industriel," *Le Figaro*.
11. Rosoff, Matt (October 12, 2011). "Jeff Bezos 'makes ordinary control freaks look like stoned hippies,' says former engineer," BusinessInsider.com.

12. Helmore, Edward (July 23, 2018). "Trumps calls Washington Post 'expensive lobbyist', reigniting war with Bezos," *Guardian*.

13. Pompeo, Joe (June 21, 2018). "'When your owner is richer than god, it's easier to get uppity': discontent at *The Washington Post* as the union targets Jeff Bezos," *Vanity Fair*.

Chapter 3: Herb Kelleher

1. Gallo, Carmine (September 10, 2013). "How Southwest and Virgin America win by putting people before profit," Forbes.com.

2. Kelleher, Herb (November 30, 2012). "I am American business: Herb Kelleher," CNBC.com. Interview available at https://www.cnbc.com/id/100000634.

3. Weber, Julie (December 02, 2015). "How Southwest Airlines hires such dedicated people," *Harvard Business Review* website.

4. Brown, Joel (January 13, 2016). "30 intelligent Herb Kelleher quotes," Addicted2Success.com.

5. Trammell, Joel (2014). *The CEO Tightrope: How to Master the Balancing Act of a Successful CEO*. Texas: Greenleaf Book Group Press.

6. Carbonara, Peter (August 31, 1996). "Hire for attitude, train for skill," *Fast Company*.

7. Rohac, Dalibor (April 24, 2013). "Conspicuous frugality: is cheap the new cool," TheUmlaut.com. Available at https://theumlaut.com/conspicuous-frugality-is-cheap-the-new-cool-1225b9fe314 (accessed December 18, 2018).

8. Yann Le Galès (June 18, 2018). "Jean-Michel Guillon, Michelin: 'nous développons la responsabilisation,'" *Le Figaro*.

9. McCarthy, Niall (May 2, 2018). "America's best large employers [Infographic]," Forbes.com.

10. Bellemare, Carole (June 12, 2018). "Jean-Michel Guillon, chez Michelin, consacré 'DRH de l'année 2018,'" *Le Figaro*.

11. Pasha, Riz (n.d.). "117 greatest Peter Drucker quotes of all time," SucceedFeed.com. Available at https://succeedfeed.com/greatest-peter-drucker-quotes (accessed December 18, 2018).

12. Lucier, Chuck (June 2004). "Herb Kelleher: the thought leader interview," *Strategy+Business*, issue 35.

13. Ignatius, Adi (March–April 2017). "We need people to lean into the future," *Harvard Business Review*.

Chapter 4: Bernard Arnault

1. LVMH 2017 Annual Report (March 2018). Available at https://r.lvmh-static.com/uploads/2018/03/lvmh_ra_2017-va.pdf.

2. Messarovitch, Yves and Bernard Arnault. (November 2000). *Bernard Arnault. La passion créative*, Paris: Plon, 67.

3. Bellemare, Carole and Caroline Beyer. (January 19, 2008). "Bernard Arnault, meilleur patron du luxe," *Le Figaro*.

4. Fox, Nick (August 12, 2011). "Think BR: 100 years of Bernbach—a creative revolution," CampaignLive.co.uk.

Chapter 5: Zhang Ruimin

1. Landler, Mark (July 23, 2000). "In China, a management Maverick builds a brand," *New York Times*.

2. Hinssen, Peter (March 2, 2017). "Innovating on the edge of chaos—getting to Haier Ground," Forbes.com.

3. Fischer, Bill, Umberto Lago, and Liu Fang (2013). *Reinventing Giants: How Chinese Global Competitor Haier Has Changed the Way Big Companies Transform*. Hoboken, NJ: John Wiley & Sons, 225.

4. Conversation with Zhang Ruimin. "For Haier's Zhang Ruimin, success means creating the future," Knowledge@ Wharton. Retrieved from knowledge.wharton.upenn.edu, April 20, 2018.

5. Fischer, Lago, and Fang. *Reinventing Giants*, 83.

6. Peter F. Drucker (2006). *Classic Drucker: Essential Wisdom of Peter Drucker from the Pages of Harvard Business Review*. New York: Harvard Business Review Press, 57.

7. Fischer, Bill, Umberto Lago, and Liu Fang (April 27, 2015). "The Haier road to growth," Strategy-Business.com.

8. Fischer, Lago, and Fang. *Reinventing Giants*, 63.

9. Cai, Peter (January 30, 2015). "Chinese innovation and the Haier model," *The Australian*.

10. Stengel, Jim (November 13, 2012). "Wisdom from the Oracle of Qingdao," Forbes.com.

Chapter 6: Jack Ma

1. Russell, Jon and Liao, Rita (November 2018). "Single's Day: China's $25 billion shopping festival explained," TechCrunch.

2. Katz, David J. (November 11, 2018). "$1 billion in sales in 85 seconds," DavidJKatz.com. Available on David J. Katz—The Alchemist blog at https://davidjkatz.com/2018/11/11/1-billion-in-85-seconds/ (accessed on December 19, 2018).

3. "Future of Payment" (November 13, 2018). "11.11—Why Singles' Day is the Asian dragon of e-commerce in the East."

Available on Wirecard blog at https://blog.wirecard.com/11-11-why-singles-day-is-the-asian-dragon-of-ecommerce-in-the-east/ (accessed on December 19, 2018).

4. Time Staff (February 28, 2000). "Jack Ma," Time .com. Available at http://content.time.com/time/world/article/0,8599,2054856,00.html (accessed on December 19, 2018).

5. Kopytoff, Verne (May 7, 2014). "Jack Ma, Alibaba's founder, in the IPO spotlight," Fortune.com.

6. Grove, Andy (1996). *Only the Paranoid Survive: How to Exploit the Crisis Points That Challenge Every Company*. New York: Currency Doubleday.

7. Smith, Craig, (December 7, 2018). "40 amazing Alipay statistics and facts (December 2018)," ExpandedRamblings.com. Available at https://expandedramblings.com/index.php/alipay-statistics/ (accessed December 19, 2018).

8. Interview of Kishore Biyani with IndiaKnowledge@Wharton. "Retailer Kishore Biyani: 'We Believe in Destroying What We Have Created." Retrieved from knowledge.wharton.upenn.edu, November 1, 2007.

9. Clark, Duncan (2016). *Alibaba: The House That Jack Ma Built*. New York: HarperCollins, 213.

10. Ibid., 210.

11. Dru, Jean-Marie (1996). *Disruption: Overturning Conventions and Shaking Up the Marketplace*. Hoboken, NJ: John Wiley & Sons, 85.

12. Tse, Edward (2015). *China's Disruptors: How Alibaba, Xiaomi, Tencent, and Other Companies Are Changing the Rules of Business*. New York: Portfolio Penguin, 40.

13. Ibid., 41.

14. "Crossing the river by feeling the stones." (July 22, 2002). *South China Morning Post*.

15. Tse, *China's Disruptors*, 105.
16. Macks Advisory (December 02, 2014). "SA and China: Singing from the Same Song Book," MacksAdvisory.com.au.
17. Carr, Austin (March 2017). "11-16 Alibaba, Tencent, Xiaomi, BBK Electronics, Huawei, Dalian Wanda for ramping up the pace for the world," *Fast Company*, issue 213, 48.
18. Ibid.
19. Tse, *China's Disruptors*, pp. 59 – 60.
20. Hahn, Lorraine, interview with Jack Ma for CNN's Talkasia (April 25, 2006). Available at: http://edition.cnn.com/2006/WORLD/asiapcf/04/24/talkasia.ma.script/index.html (accessed December 19, 2018).
21. Tse, *China's Disruptors*, 37
22. Wang, Helen H., (July 2, 2014). "Alibaba Saga II: Meg Whitman unexpectedly met her match," Forbes.com.

PART TWO: Disruptive Business Thinking

1. Dru, Jean-Marie (2007). *How Disruption Brought Order*. New York: Palgrave Macmillan.
2. Yueh, Jedidiah (2017). *Disrupt or Die: What the World Needs to Learn from Silicon Valley to Survive the Digital Era*. Austin: Lioncrest Publishing.

Chapter 7: Jim Collins

1. Collins, Jim (2001). *Good to Great: Why Some Companies Make the Leap . . . and Others Don't*. New York: Collins Business.
2. Collins, Jim and Jerry I. Porras, (1994). *Built to Last: Successful Habits of Visionary Companies*. New York: HarperCollins Publishers.

3. The One Club for Creativity. "Jay Chiat. Inducted: 1994," OneClub.org. Available at https://www.oneclub.org/hall-of-fame/-bio/jay-chiat (accessed on December 19, 2018).

4. Collins, *Good to Great*, 98.

5. Koehn, Nancy (October 2017). Presentation to TBWA executives at Management Network Meeting in Milan.

6. News Blog (news.pg.com, June 27, 2012). "Pampers: The Birth of P&G's First 10-Billion-Dollar Brand."

7. "Our vision." Available at https://www.dove.com/us/en/stories/about-dove/our-vision.html (accessed on December 19, 2018).

8. Sidle, Clinton C., (2005). *The Leadership Wheel: Five Steps for Achieving Individual and Organizational Greatness*. New York: St. Martin's Press, p. 174.

9. Ibid.

10. Stein, Jean (Spring 1956). "William Faulkner, The Art of Fiction N° 12," *The Paris Review*, issue 12.

11. Fitzgerald, F. Scott (March 7, 2017). "Part I: The Crack-Up," Esquire.com. Originally published as a three-part series in the February, March, and April 1936 issues of *Esquire*.

12. Smith, Wendy K., Marianne W. Lewis, and Michael L. Tushman (May 2016). "'Both/And' Leadership," *Harvard Business Review*.

13. Chapuis, Dominique and David Barroux. (June 16, 2017). "Jean-Paul Agon: 'Nous allons passer dans un nouveau monde,'" *Le Sochos*.

14. Isaacson, Walter (2011). *Steve Jobs*. New York: Simon & Schuster, 567.

15. Thiel, Peter and Blake Masters (2015). *Zero to One: Notes on Start-Ups, or How to Build the Future*. London: Virgin Books.

16. Dylan, Bob (1964). "My Back Pages," song from the album *Another Side of Bob Dylan*.

17. Ponomarev, L.I. (1993). *The Quantum Dice*. United Kingdom: IOP Publishing Ltd, 75.

Chapter 8: Clayton Christensen

1. Christensen, Clayton M., (1997). *The Innovator's Dilemma: When New Technologies Cause Great Firms to Fail.* Massachusetts: Harvard Business Review Press.

2. Christensen Clayton M., and Joseph L. Bower (January-February 1995 issue). "Disruptive Technologies: Catching The Wave," *Harvard Business Review*.

3. Kuhn, Thomas Samuel (1962). *The Structure of Scientific Revolutions*. Chicago: University of Chicago Press.

4. Crain, Rance (September 12, 2016). "Jean-Marie Dru on Why Disruption isn't Destruction," AdAge.com.

5. Christensen, "Disruptive Technologies," preface.

6. Lepore, Jill (June 23, 2014). "The Disruption Machine. What the gospel of innovation gets wrong," *The New Yorker*.

7. King, Andrew A. and Baljir Baatartogtokh. (September 15, 2015). "How Useful is the Theory of Disruptive Innovation?" *MIT Sloan Management Review*.

8. Dru, Jean-Marie (December 17, 2015). "A Counterargument to Clayton Christensen's Definition of True Disruption," Forbes.com.

Chapter 9: Jedidiah Yueh

1. Ip, Greg (December 20, 2016). "The Economy's Hidden Problem: We're Out of Big Ideas," *Wall Street Journal*.

2. Bloom, Nicholas Jones, Chad Jones, John Van Reenen, and Michael Webb (December 20, 2017). "Great Ideas Are Getting Harder to Find," Sloan.MIT.edu.
3. Dru, Jean-Marie (2015). *The Ways to New: 15 Paths to Disruptive Innovation*. Hoboken, NJ: John Wiley & Sons.
4. Yueh, Jedidiah (2017). *Disrupt or Die: What the World Needs to Learn from Silicon Valley to Survive the Digital Era*. Austin: Lioncrest Publishing, 28.
5. Ibid., 22.
6. Ibid., 21.
7. Ibid., 122.
8. Huijgen, Annelot and Ivan Letessier (June 15, 2016). "Jeff Immelt: Internet crée une revolution industrielle," *Le Figaro*.
9. Yueh, *Disrupt or Die*, 59.
10. Yueh, *Disrupt or Die*, 99.
11. Henke, Nicolaus, Ari Libarikian, and Bill Wiseman (October 2016). "Straight talk about big data," *McKinsey Quarterly*, Available at https://www.mckinsey.com/business-functions/digital-mckinsey/our-insights/straight-talk-about-big-data (accessed December 22, 2018).
12. Ibid.
13. Collins, Jim (2009). *How the Mighty Fall: And Why Some Companies Never Give In*. New York: JimCollins.
14. Yueh, *Disrupt or Die*, 73.
15. Ibid., 75.
16. Ibid., 233.
17. Yoon, Eddie (September 26, 2011). "Category creation is the ultimate growth strategy," *Harvard Business Review*.
18. Thiel, Peter and Blake Masters (2014). *Zero to One: Notes on Start-Ups, or How to Build the Future*. New York: Crown Business. 35.
19. Ibid., 34.
20. Ibid., 2, 20, 23, 130, 138.

21. Zinni, Anthony, Ronald Keys, and Frank Bowman (October 31, 2014). "US military refuses to be 'too late' on climate change," *News Tribune*.

PART THREE: Disruptive Corporate Culture

1. Entrepreneur. "Corporate Culture," Small Business Encyclopedia. Available at https://www.entrepreneur.com/encyclopedia.
2. Groysberg, Boris, Jeremiah Lee, Jesse Price, and Yo-Jud J. Cheng (January–February 2018). "The leader's guide to corporate culture." *Harvard Business Review* 96(01), 44–52.
3. Ulrcih, Dave and Wayne Brockbank (March 18, 2016). "Your company culture can't be disconnected from your customers," *Harvard Business Review*.
4. Dru, Jean-Marie (May 25, 2007). "Culture et compétitivité," *Les Echos*.
5. Kotter, John P., and James L. Heskett, (1992). *Corporate Culture and Performance*. New York: Free Press.
6. Maister, David H. (2003). *Practice What You Preach: What Managers Must Do to Create a High Achievement Culture*. New York: Free Press.

Chapter 10: Sergey Brin and Larry Page

1. Page, Larry and Sergey Brin (April 29, 2004). 2004 Founders' IPO Letter. "'An owner's manual' for Google's shareholders," *New York Times*. From the S-1 Registration Statement filed with Securities and Exchange Commission.
2. Friedman, Thomas L. (February 22, 2014). "How to get a job at Google," *New York Times*.

3. Ibid.
4. Blackiston, Mary (January 19, 2018). "What every company can learn from Google's company culture," SuccessAgency .com.
5. Vozza, Stephanie (April 28, 2015). "What the most successful employers know," *Fast Company* website.
6. Yueh, Jedidiah (2017). *Disrupt or Die: What the World Needs to Learn from Silicon Valley to Survive the Digital Era*. Austin: Lioncrest Publishing, 106.
7. Ibid., 107.

Chapter 11: Patty McCord

1. Moyer, Justin Wm. (October 5, 2015). "Alphabet, now Google's overlord, ditches 'don't be evil' for 'do the right thing,'" *Washington Post*.
2. Ibid.
3. Netflix. "Netflix Culture." Available at https://jobs.netflix .com/culture (accessed on December 24, 2018).
4. Hass, Nancy (January 29, 2013). "And the award for the next HBO goes to . . . ," *GQ* online.
5. Turco, Catherine J. (2016). *The Conversational Firm: Rethinking Bureaucracy in the Age of Social Media*. New York: Columbia University Press.
6. Quito, Anne (April 19, 2018). "Netflix's CEO says there are months when he doesn't have to make a single decision," *Quartz*.
7. Chris Anderson (April 2018). "Reed Hastings: how Netflix changed entertainment . . . and where it's headed," TED Talk. Available at https://www.ted.com/talks/reed_hastings_

how_netflix_changed_entertainment_and_where_it_s_
headed (accessed on December 24, 2018).

8. McCord, Patty (January–February 2014). "How Netflix reinvented HR," *Harvard Business Review*.

9. Ibid.

10. Denning, Stephanie (October 26, 2018). "The Netflix pressure-cooker: a culture that drives performance," Forbes .com

11. Wooldridge, Adrian (2015). *The Great Disruption: How Business Is Coping with Turbulent Times*. London: The Economist.

12. Singh, Aman (August 17, 2000). "At Netflix, manic performance gets unlimited time off," CNBC.com.

Chapter 12: The Disruption Company

1. Coleman, John (May 6, 2013). "Six components of a great corporate culture," *Harvard Business Review* online.

2. Hunt, John. (2009). *The Art of the Idea: And How It Can Change Your Life*. New York: PowerHouse Books.

3. Coleman, "Six components of a great corporate culture.".

4. Cioran, E. M. (1991). *Anathemas and Admirations*. New York: Arcade Publishing.

5. Taylor, William C., and Polly G. Labarre (2006). *Mavericks at Work: Why the Most Original Minds in Business Win*. New York: William Morrow.

6. Day, Annicken R. (January 29, 2017). "When culture becomes a strategy for growth," *Huffington Post*.

7. Gerstner, Louis V. Jr. (2002). *Who Says Elephants Can't Dance?* New York: Harper Business.

PART FOUR: Disruptive Brand Building

1. Branson, Richard (2009). *Business Stripped Bare: Adventures of a Global Entrepreneur.* London: Virgin Books, p.68.
2. Simon, Mario (2010). "Millward Brown Point of View. Brand: The New Business Leadership," MillwardBrown.com.
3. "What are brands for?" (August 30, 2014). *The Economist.*

Chapter 13: Marc Pritchard

1. Vizard, Sarah (October 4, 2017). "'Marketer of the Year' Marc Pritchard on his quest for transparency," *Marketing Week.*
2. Kumar, Rajesh B. (2018). *Wealth Creation in the World's Largest Mergers and Acquisitions: Integrated Case Studies.* Switzerland: Springer, 246.
3. Nicolaou, Anna (July 18, 2017). "P&G's chief executive wrestles with changing an 'insular' culture," *Financial Times.*
4. Johnson, Lauren (September 4, 2017). "DMEXCO 2017: The Standard Bearer P&G's Marc Pritchard raised a red flag on transparency and now the industry is taking action." *Adweek.*
5. Vizard, Sarah (September 14, 2017). "Marc Pritchard: 2017 is the year the bloom came off the rose for digital media," *Marketing Week.*
6. Vizard, Sarah (March 1, 2018). "P&G's Marc Pritchard calls for an end to the 'archaic *Mad Men* model,'" *Marketing Week.*
7. Roderick, Leonie (January 30, 2017). "P&G issues call to arms to ad industry over 'antiquated' media buying," *Marketing Week.*

8. Handley, Lucy (January 31, 2017). "Procter & Gamble chief marketer slams 'crappy media supply chain,' urges marketers to act," CNBC.com

9. "Procter & Gamble chief issues powerful media transparency rallying cry," (January 30, 2017). CampaignLive.co.uk. Marc Pritchard's full speech on January 29, 2017, at U.S. IAB Annual Leadership meeting in Florida available at https://www.campaignlive.co.uk/article/procter-gamble-chief-issues-powerful-media-transparency-rallying-cry/1422599 (accessed on December 26, 2018).

10. Ritson, Mark (January 31, 2017). "P&G's Marc Pritchard has made the biggest marketing speech for 20 years," *Marketing Week*.

11. Vizard, "'Marketer of the Year.'"

12. Nail, Jim (March 2, 2018). "'Three things I never expected Marc Pritchard to say . . . but every marketer needs to hear," Forbes.com.

13. Pearl, Diana (November 6, 2018). "7 takeaways from Adweek's conversation with P&G Chief Brand Officer Marc Pritchard," *AdWeek*.

14. Pritchard, Marc (February 10, 2012). "FY 12/13 Digital/eCommerce Brand Building Guidance," Procter &Gamble memo.

15. News Media Association (September 14, 2017). "P&G questions value of 'annoying' two-second digital ads," NewsMediaUK.org.

16. Dru, Jean-Marie (1984). *Le Saut Créatif: Ces idées publicitaires qui valent des milliards.* Paris: Jean-Claude Lattès.

17. "Procter & Gamble chief issues powerful media transparency rallying cry." (January 30, 2017). *Campaign*. Op. cit.

18. Parpis, Eleftheria (October 22, 2016). "P&G's Marc Pritchard challenges brands to 'invest in agencies," *Campaign* website.

19. Mortimer, Natalie (February 26, 2014). "'The brands that will thrive in the coming years are the ones that have a purpose beyond profit' says Richard Branson," TheDrum .com.

20. Procter & Gamble (n.d.). "Purpose and People," PG.com. Available at https://www.pg.com/en_AP/company/purpose_people/index.shtml (accessed on December 26, 2018).

21. "Girl Empowerment throughout the world with Always," (n.d.). Always.com. Available at https://always.com/en-us/about-us/girl-empowerment-throughout-the-world-with-always (accessed on December 26, 2018).

22. Laborde, Olivier (2017). *Innover Ou Disparaître: Le Lab Pour Remetrre L'Innovation Au Coeur de L'Entreprise.* Paris: Dunod.

23. Battelle, John (April 2018). "The Biggest Voice in Advertising Finds Its Purpose," Shift.Newco.co.

24. Reingold, Jennifer and Doris Burke. (February 8, 2013). "Can Procter & Gamble CEO Bob McDonald hang on?" *Fortune* website.

25. Crain, Rance (March 6, 2013). "Is the era of purpose-driven ads (finally) over?" *Ad Age.*

26. Sweeney, Erica (April 19, 2018). "Study: Brands with a purpose grow 2x faster than others," MarketingDive .com. Kantar Consulting full report "Purpose 2020. Igniting Purpose-Led Growth" available at https://consulting.kantar.com/wp-content/uploads/2018/07/Real-Initiative-for-Growth-Purpose-2020.pdf (accessed December 26, 2018).

Chapter 14: Brian Chesky

1. Emerson, Lincoln (2018). *Brian Chesky: The Life & Mind of the Airbnb Founder from Debt to Darling.* Self-published, 20.
2. Ibid., 46.
3. Safian, Robert (April 18, 2017). "What Airbnb has discovered about building a lasting brand," *Fast Company.*
4. Ibid.
5. Ibid.
6. Airbnb (2016). "Don't Go There. Live There." Airbnb's brand campaign launched in 2016. Video available at https://adage.com/creativity/work/dont-go-there-live-there/46533 (accesssed on December 26, 2018).
7. Safian, "What Airbnb has discovered about building a lasting brand."
8. Airbnb (2015). "No borders." Airbnb's campaign launched in 2015. Video available at https://fr.adforum.com/creative-work/ad/player/34527954/no-borders/airbnb (accesssed on December 26, 2018).
9. Olson, Adam (April 8, 2015). "Airbnb marks brand's foray into Cuba with new campaign," CampaignLive.co.uk.
10. Ho, Nancy (June 1, 2017) "Airbnb uses big data and machine learning to enhance user experience," CW.com.hk.
11. Horst, Peter and Robert Duboff (November 2015). "Don't let big data bury your brand," *Harvard Business Review,* 78–84, 86.
12. Bazilian, Emma (September 27, 2012). "Ad of the Day: Nike. Today's kids, destined to die younger, talk about what they'd do with five extra years," *Adweek.*
13. Nike's "Designed to Move" campaign. Video available at http://fr.designedtomove.org (accesssed on December 26, 2018).

14. Yueh, Jedidiah (2017). *Disrupt or Die: What the World Needs to Learn from Silicon Valley to Survive the Digital Era.* Austin: Lioncrest Publishing, 197.
15. Ibid., 198.
16. Kantar Consulting (2018). *Purpose 2020: Igniting Purpose-Led Growth.* Available at: https://consulting.kantar.com/wp-content/uploads/2018/07/Real-Initiative-for-Growth-Purpose-2020.pdf (accessed January 29, 2018).

Chapter 15: Lee Clow

1. Nudd, Tim (April 13, 2011). "Apple's 'Get a Mac,' the complete campaign," *AdWeek.*
2. Apple. "Here's to the Crazy Ones," commercial. Video available at https://www.youtube.com/watch?v=cFEarBzelBs (accessed on December 26, 2018).
3. Creamer, Matthew (October 24, 2011). "Isaacson's book portrays Jobs as everything an agency would want in a client," *Ad Age.*
4. Pritchard, Marc (October 14, 2010). "P&G: Empowering Brands Through Design And Innovation." Speech at the 2010 ANA Annual Conference in Florida.
5. Nike (2018). "Dream Crazy" commercial. Video available at https://www.forbes.com/sites/derekrucker/2018/09/06/nike-dream-crazy-a-rich-opportunity-to-learn-about-brand-management-in-the-digital-age/#6514c4443c4b (accessed on December 27, 2018).
6. [Value of Nike Brand/Market Capitalization of Nike Inc.] x 100 = [US$32 billion/ US$115,66 billion] x 100 = 27,7%. Value of Nike Brand sourced from http://brandfinance.com/news/press-releases/most-valuable-apparel-brand-

nike-just-does-it-again/Market Capitalization of Nike Inc. on December 28, 2018 sourced from https://ycharts.com/companies/NKE/market_cap

7. Avi, Dan (October 23, 2016). "P&G's Marc Pritchard on avoiding the 'crap trap' in advertising," Forbes.com.

8. The Gunn Report and IPA Databank (June 2011). *The Link between Creativity and Effectiveness. The Growing Imperative to Embrace Creativity. More Findings from the Gunn Report and the IPA Databank.* London: Institute of Practitioners in Advertising. Available at https://adfx.ie/upload/files/1466161111_Creativity_and_Effectiveness.pdf (accessed on December 27, 2018).

9. Perrey, Jesko, Nicola Wagener, and Carsten Wallmann, (October 4, 2007). ADC/McKinsey Study "Der Code erfolgreicher Werbung."

10. Brodherson, Marc, Jason Heller, Jesko Perrey, and David Remley (2017). "Creativity's Bottom Line: How Winning Companies Turn Creativity into Business Value and Growth," McKinsey.com.

11. ADA and McKinsey (2006). "Creativity Is an Advertiser's Best Bet."

12. Clow, Lee (October 17, 2009). "Mad Men: Sell It" panel discussion, New Yorker Festival, held at City Winery, New York, NY.

PART FIVE: Disruptive Social Purpose

1. "Madam C. J. Walker: from poverty to prosperity," (October 10, 2008). *Entrepreneur* online.

2. Gates, Henry Louis Jr. (December 7, 1998). "Madam C. J. Walker: her crusade. A black woman's hair-care empire set a style and smashed barriers," *Time* magazine.

3. Bundles, A'Lelia (December 19, 2018). "Madam C. J. Walker: American businesswoman and philanthropist," *Encyclopaedia Britannica* online.

4. Anderson, Niele (June 20, 2017). "Madam C. J. Walker: An American Legacy of Success, Love and Prosperity," Niele's Daily Top 10 website.

5. Bundles, "Madam C. J. Walker."

6. Michals, Debra (2015). "Madam C. J. Walker (1867–1919)," National Women's History Museum website (www.WomensHistory.org).

7. Green, Duncan (September 20, 2016). "The World's Top 100 Economies: 31 Countries; 69 Corporations," World Bank blog.

8. Nielsen (October 12, 2015). ("Consumer-Goods' Brands That Demonstrate Commitment to Sustainability Outperform Those That Don't," *2015 Nielsen Global Corporate Sustainability Report.*

9. Bowen, Howard R. (1953). *Social Responsibilities of the Businessman.* Iowa: University of Iowa Press.

10. Caulkins, Doug (December 20, 2013). "President Howard Bowen & Corporate Social Responsibility," Grinnell.edu.

11. Morse, Gardiner (July 21, 2014). "Reinventing the chief marketing officer: an interview with Unilever CMO Keith Weed," *Harvard Business Review.*

12. Friedman, Milton (September 13, 1970). "The social responsibility of business is to increase its profits: a doctrine by Milton Friedman." *New York Times Magazine.*

13. Porter, Michael E. and Mark R. Kramer (January–February 2011). "The big idea: creating shared value. How to reinvent capitalism and unleash a wave of innovation and growth," *Harvard Business Review* 89 (1–2), pp. 62–77.

14. Ibid.

15. Safian, Robert, (March 2014) "Twelve innovation lessons for 2014," (*Fast Company*, issue 183, March 2014).

Chapter 16: Oprah Winfrey

1. White paper published by TBWA\Chiat\Day and Airbnb. "How to create loyalty beyond reason. The what, why and how of building an iconic brand." Retrieved from https://cdn2.hubspot.net/hubfs/320867/Airbnb-Whitepaper.pdf?t=1522417508619, March 25, 2019.

2. Matz, Katherine and Leto, Ellen (April 3, 2009). "The Big O: How Oprah Winfrey Built Her Brand." Retrieved from Public Relations Problems and Cases: April 2009. Available at http://psucomm473.blogspot.com/2009/04/ (accessed March 25, 2019).

3. Ibid.

4. Clemett, Lauren, "Top 27 Personal Branding Lessons from Oprah Winfrey." Ultimatebusinesspropellor.com. Available at https://ultimatebusinesspropellor.com/top-27-personal-branding-lessons-oprah-winfrey/ (accessed March 25, 2019).

5. Causay, T.R., (January 3, 2017). "Oprah's 15 Tips To Living Your Best Life." Blackdoctor.org

6. Sohn, Emily (May 26, 2011). "How Oprah Winfrey changed America." NBCNEWS.com.

7. Gonzalez, Sandra (January 10, 2018). "Oprah Winfrey: 'For too long women have not been heard or believed.'" CNN.com

8. UNICEF (November 2015). "For every child, a fair chance: The promise of equity." Available at https://www.unicef.org/publications/index_86269.html (accessed March 25, 2019).

9. Decurtis, Anthony (June 5, 2017). "Not a Businessman – a Business, Man." Bestlifeonline.com.

10. Pofeldt, Elaine (March 21, 2018). "3 ways to transform your 1-person business into a $1 million operation." Marketwatch.com

11. Peters, Tom (August 31, 1997). "The Brand Called You." August-September 1997 issue, *Fast Company*.
12. Pofeldt, Elaine (April 29, 2018). "How To Build Your Own Million-Dollar, One-Person Business: Advice From The Front Lines. *Forbes* website.
13. Spangler, Todd (March 3, 2015). "Millennials Find You Tube Content More Entertaining, Relatable Than TV: Study." *Variety* website.
14. Ault, Susanne (July 23, 2015). "Digital Star Popularity Grows Versus Mainstream Celebrities." *Variety* website.
15. Pofeldt, Elaine (October 17, 2017). "Are We Ready For A Workforce That is 50% Freelance?" *Forbes* website.
16. Clemett, Lauren, Op. cit.

Chapter 17: Arianna Huffington

1. The Observers (August 25, 2016). "Building homes out of recycled plastic in Colombia." Available at https://observers.france24.com/en/20160815-colombia-building-homes-recycled-plastic-displaced (accessed March 25, 2019).
2. Scholfield, Andrew (October 1-2, 2015). "Arianna Huffington. The Brave New World of the 'New Media,'" Nordic Business Forum 2015 Executive Summary, *Nordic Business Report*.
3. Ibid.
4. Abramson, Jill (February 2019). *Merchants of Truth: Inside the News Revolution*. London: Bodley Head, 72.
5. Keller, Bill (March 10, 2011). "All the Aggregation That's Fit to Aggregate." *The New York Times Magazine* website.
6. Abramson, Jill (February 2019). Op. cit.

7. Davis, Elmer H. (1921). *History of the New York Times, 1851 – 1921* (New York: New York Times) 232.

8. Butler, Susan B. (June 10, 2014). "Gender Equality= Men+Women Working Together." *Huffington Post*.

9. Ibid.

10. Bureau of Labor Statistics Reports (November 2017). "Women in the labor force: a databook." Available at https://www.bls.gov/opub/reports/womens-databook/2017/home.htm (accessed March 26, 2019).

11. Capperella, Joel (February 10, 2013). "Why the Most Disruptive Force in Tech Is Women." *Huffington Post*.

12. Editorial Team (February 11, 2019). "'Give up the delusion that burnout is the inevitable cost of success': Arianna Huffington." People Matters website.

13. Huffington, Arianna (August 17, 2018). "An Open Letter to Elon Musk. You're demonstrating a wildly outdated, anti-scientific and horribly inefficient way of using human energy." Available at https://thriveglobal.com/stories/open-letter-elon-musk/ (accessed March 26, 2019).

14. Lu, Jane (June 12, 2018). "Arianna Huffington And Jennifer Breithaupt: Achieve More By Going Offline." *Digitalist Magazine* online.

15. Hunt, Vivian, Dennis Layton and Sara Prince (January 2015). "Why diversity matters," McKinsey. Report available at https://www.mckinsey.com/business-functions/organization/our-insights/why-diversity-matters (accessed March 26, 2019).

16. Manyika James, Anu Madgavkar, and Jonathan Woetzel (September 24, 2015). "The Power of Gender Parity." *Huffington Post*.

Chapter 18: Paul Polman

1. Cunningham, Lillian (May 21, 2015). "The tao of Paul Polman," *Washington Post.*
2. PricewaterhouseCoopers. *Millennials at Work: Reshaping the Workplace.* Available at https://www.pwc.com/co/es/publicaciones/assets/millennials-at-work.pdf (accessed on December 30, 2018).
3. "Unilever: In search of the good business," (August 9, 2014), Economist.com.
4. Eleftheriou-Smith, Loulla-Mae (November 23, 2011). "Unilever draws up 'Five Levers for Change' strategy," *Campaign.*
5. Schawbel, Dan (November 21, 2017). "Unilever's Paul Polman: why today's leaders need to commit to a purpose," Forbes.com.
6. "Unilever: In search of the good business." (August 9, 2014), *The Economist.*
7. Weber Shandwick and KRC Research (March–April 2017). *CEO Activism in 2017: High Noon in the C-Suite.*
8. McGregor, Jena and Elizabeth Dwoskin(February 17, 2017). "The cost of silence: why more CEOs are speaking out in the Trump era," *Washington Post.*
9. Brunner, Rob (April 2017). "How Chobani founder Hamid Ulukaya is winning America's culture war," *Fast Company,* issue 214, 62.
10. Ibid.
11. Fast Company (March 2017). "The world's 50 most innovative companies. Chobani: for stirring it up in the grocery store." *Fast Company,* issue 213, 44.
12. Fink, Larry. (2018). "A Sense of Purpose: Annual Letter to CEOs," BlackRock. Available at https://www.blackrock.

com/corporate/investor-relations/larry-fink-ceo-letter (accessed on December 31, 2018).

13. Sorkin, Andrew Ross (January 15, 2018). "BlackRock's message: contribute to society, or risk losing our support," *New York Times*.

14. Fink, "A Sense of Purpose."

Chapter 19: Emmanuel Faber

1. Mousli, Marc (May 2014). "Le discours de Marseille d'Antoine Riboud," *L'Économie Politique* magazine, no. 62.

2. Riboud, Antoine (October 25, 1972). "Croissance et Qualité de vie," speech given at the Assises nationales of CNPF. Available at http://go-management.fr/wp-content/uploads/2016/07/Discours-dAntoine-Riboud-aux-Assises-nationales-du-CNPF-le-25-octobre-1972-à-Marseille.pdf (accessed January 1, 2019).

3. Ibid.

4. Faber, Emmanuel (2011). *Chemins de traverse: vivre l'économie autrement*. Paris: Albin Michel, 60.

5. Ibid., 32.

6. Ibid., 147.

7. Ibid., 120.

8. Danone (n.d.). "Notre Vision. Danone, One Planet, One Health," Danone.com. Available at https://www.danone.com/fr/about-danone/sustainable-value-creation/our-vision.html (accessed January 1, 2019).

9. Mougey, Amélie (January 26, 2015). "Une pomme de 1950 équivaut à 100 pommes aujourd'hui," NouveLObs.com.

10. Flallo, Laurent (June 22, 2017). "Danone, les ferments d'une revolution," *Les Echos*.

11. Pralahad, C. K. and Stuart, Hart L. (2002). "The fortune at the bottom of the pyramid," *Strategy+Business*, issue 26.

12. Faber, *Chemins de traverse*, 87.

13. Hussain, Mehdi, Abdul Hannan Chowdhury, and Bashir Hussain (July 2012). "Sweet and sours of social businesses: a case study on Grameeen Danone Foods Ltd," *World Journal of Social Sciences* 2(4), 256–266.

14. Prasso, Sheridan (February 2007). "Saving the world with a cup of yogurt," *Fortune* magazine 155(2).

15. Faber, *Chemins de traverse*, 107.

16. *The Economist* (January 28, 2017). "Briefing multinationals: The retreat of the global company," 18–22.

17. Cougard, Marie-Josée, Emmanuel Grasland, and David Barroux (December 1, 2017). "Emmanuel Faber: 'la revolution de l'alimentation se fera avec les marques locales,'" *Les Echos*.

18. Faber, *Chemins de traverse*, 108.

Chapter 20: Marc Benioff and Suzanne DiBianca

1. Salesforce (n.d.). "Take the Pledge. Pledge 1%. 1-1-1 Philanthropic Model," Salesforce.com. Available at https://www.salesforce.org/pledge-1/ (accessed on January 1, 2019).

2. Salesforce (April 18, 2017). "1% to change the world." Video available at https://www.youtube.com/watch?v=YApfNp4tG1g (accessed on January 1, 2019).

3. Pledge 1% (May 3, 2018). "Pledge 1% Announces 5,000 Members in Over 100 Countries at Collision," PledgeItForward.today.

4. Harlow, Poppy (June 11, 2015). "Benioff: 'The business of business is not business," CNN Money. Video available at https://money.cnn.com/video/technology/2015/06/11/

marc-benioff-salesforce-ceo-responsibility.cnnmoney/
index.html (accessed on January 1, 2019).

5. Wicks, Jason (2018). *The Price of Profit: Rethinking Corporate Social Responsibility*. New York: Independently Published, 24

6. *Leaders* magazine (2012). "Shaping the future. Share the model. An interview with Marc Benioff, Chairman and Chief Executive Officer, Salesforce.com," 35(2). Available at http://www.leadersmag.com/issues/2012.2_Apr/PDFs/ LEADERS-Marc-Benioff-salesforcecom.pdf (accessed on January 2, 2019).

7. Zakaras, Michael (July 21, 2016). "Salesforce Chief Philanthropy Officer Suzanne DiBianca wants all companies to drive social change," Forbes.com.

8. United Nations (May 28, 2015). "'We are the first generation that can end poverty, the last that can end climate change,' Secretary-General stresses at university ceremony," press release. Available at https://www.un.org/press/en/2015/ sgsm16800.doc.htm (accessed on January 2, 2019).

Index